WALES:
ENGLAND'S
COLONY?

Martin Johnes grew up in Pembrokeshire, lives in Cardiff and works at Swansea University, where he is Professor of Modern History. His research explores questions of identity in sport, politics and popular culture and has included studies of football, archery, popular music, Christmas, disasters, and local government. His other books include *Wales since 1939* (2012) and *A History of Sport in Wales* (2005), and, with Iain McLean, *Aberfan: Government and Disasters* (2000). He can be found on Twitter @martinjohnes.

WALES: ENGLAND'S COLONY?

The Conquest, Assimilation and Re-creation of Wales

Martin Johnes

Parthian, Cardigan SA43 1ED
www.parthianbooks.com
First published in 2019
Reprinted 2020, 2021, 2022
© Martin Johnes
ISBN 978-1-912681-41-9
Cover design: www.theundercard.com
Edited by Dai Smith
Typeset by Elaine Sharples
Printed and bound by 4edge
Published with the financial support of the Welsh Books Council
The Modern Wales series receives support from the Rhys Davies Trust
A cataloguing record for this book is available from the British Library.

CONTENTS

PREFACE

There are many different ways to tell the history of Wales and its relationship with England. This book is my attempt.

The project's roots lie with my own. I grew up in a small village in north Pembrokeshire, where I learned about being an outsider and an insider. My family were not local and we spoke English at home. At school and at play, I spoke Welsh. We went to church not chapel, although *Top of the Pops* was more my gospel. I had a teacher, Mr David Llewellyn, who encouraged my curiosity and instilled in me a sense that the local mattered, whether that be a slate quarry or a prehistoric monument. He also seemed in no doubt that Wales was worth fighting for. There was probably much to fight about, although politics was not much discussed in front of children. Margaret Thatcher was prime minister. Coal mines were something only visible on the news, although trucks of coal were seen on trips east during the long strike that I did not really understand. My mother worked for the National Health Service. My father was a self-employed engineer, working with farmers, dairies, small factories, and the oil refineries in the south. Swansea City were briefly in the first division, although I rarely saw them play. Everyone seemed obsessed by rugby, although Wales were not the team they had been in the seventies. The hills and sea were nearby and the landscape was littered with castles. No one went abroad, or to north Wales. We are all products of our upbringing and part of the battle of writing history is realising this; another part is trying to overcome it. The reader can decide my success or otherwise.

Thanks are due to all the following. Max Davies, Tim Green, Richard Longstaff and Amy Quant for translating the book into something that would work on screen. Richard Davies and all at Parthian for putting it on paper (and doing so quickly). Dai Smith for his editing and reminders to tell it how it was and not how we want it to be. Chris Williams for helping me become a historian in the first place. For advice and assistance: Nick Barnett, Sam Blaxland, Emma Cavell, Madeleine Gray, Tomás Irish, Leighton James, Bethan Jenkins, Simon John, Alex Langlands, Louise Miskell, Teresa Phipps, Nigel Pollard, Dan Power, Matthew Stevens, David Turner, and Daniel Williams. My students, past and present, for reminding me that teaching is a two-way process, and one much better captured by the Welsh word dysgu. Heather Moyes for attempting to curb any polemic and for living with the project with relative good humour. Bethan and Anwen Johnes for doing what teenage daughters do. And finally, the UK's top politicians for distracting my writing with their attempts to destroy what the past bequeathed them.

Diolch i chi gyd.

Martin Johnes
Cardiff & Swansea

INTRODUCTION

Anyone looking up Wales in the 1888 edition of *Encyclopaedia Britannica* would have found the simple entry 'See England'. In contrast, had they turned to the entry for Scotland they would have found a passage running to seventy-four pages. The phrase 'For Wales see England' has become notorious. For some, it sums up how Wales is invisible to the wider world. More commonly, it is seen as an example of English arrogance and a tendency to dismiss the idea of Wales as a separate nation. Both these things have sometimes been true, but the entry also hints unintentionally at a different truth: understanding Wales without looking at England is impossible. From the very beginnings of Wales, its people have defined themselves against their large neighbour. As this book shows, that relationship has not only defined what it has meant to be Welsh, it has also been central to making and defining Wales as a nation.

This might be an uncomfortable idea since it could suggest that somehow Wales is not a nation in its own right. But all nations look to others to define themselves. As historian Linda Colley has put it, 'Men and women decide who they are by reference to who and what they are not'. The sense of difference from someone or something else creates a common bond amongst what are often disparate people, and their loose sense of unity is turned into something more visceral. In some cases, an unequal relationship makes the sense of difference very

1

powerful and puts it at the heart of an identity. Canada, for example, cannot be understood without reference to its relationship with the USA: so much of its culture and politics is defined by consciously being different to the country to its south. But even for nations not overshadowed by a powerful neighbour, a sense of difference from others is often central. The USA's belief in its importance and power over other nations illustrates that. So, too, does the UK's 2016 vote in favour of leaving the EU. Yet, as both these examples illustrate, a nation's sense of difference can owe more to imagination than reality.

The idea that Wales has been defined by its relationship with England is also uncomfortable because the relationship between the two nations has not always been a happy one and never one between equals. Wales was England's first colony. Its conquest was by military force and led to a process of colonisation whereby the Welsh were denied what today would be called civil rights. It was accompanied by implantations of foreigners, the abolition of some traditional customs, and the introduction of new taxes. The phrase 'imperial exploitation' might be a modern one but it is applicable to medieval Wales. England then formally annexed Wales through what today are known as the Acts of Union. Its separate legal status came to an end and assimilation into England gathered pace. Skip forward a few centuries and an enquiry into Welsh education revealed hostile prejudices towards the Welsh language and the Welsh character, illustrating how political assimilation had not brought cultural equality. Some schools in the nineteenth century physically punished children for speaking Welsh, leading to subsequent accusations that the language was beaten out of children. In the 1950s and 60s, there was an outcry when a rural Welsh-speaking community was destroyed to supply an English city with water. There was anger too at governance from London when Welsh industry went into retreat. In the 1980s, a year-long miners' strike across the UK was widely interpreted within Wales as a desperate struggle to keep the Welsh coal industry alive in the face of English indifference. Some even maintain that the coal industry typifies how Wales has been robbed of its natural resources to feed the English economy. If this is the sum of Wales' history, it is little wonder that some want to throw off 'the English yoke'.

When we sit under a tree and gaze upwards, our eyes are drawn to the gaps where the sunlight shines through and not the mass of leaves closer to us. Much the same is true of gazing at the Welsh national past. The occasions of oppression and injustice stand out, diverting our attention from the much wider and more mundane mass of more harmonious relations. As historian Margaret MacMillan has pointed out, 'It is all too easy to rummage through the past and find nothing but a list of grievances'. Welsh history is more complicated than a list of things the 'nasty' English did and none of the above examples were quite as straightforward as the headlines might suggest. The past is just too messy to reduce to stories of 'goodies' and 'baddies'. Even the central story of conquest is not all it might seem because medieval Wales was not a single political unit but a collection of rival kingdoms at war with each other as much as with England. Moreover, some of the Welsh had fought with the English rather than against them. Nor are the heroes of medieval Welsh history all they might first seem to be. Llywelyn Fawr, perhaps the greatest of the independent Welsh princes, and Owain Glyndŵr, the leader of Wales' great rebellion, both also served in English armies. Glyndŵr's revolt may still inspire patriots but it actually inflicted considerable economic misery on his people and nation. Nor are tales of exploitation any simpler. At the height of Wales' economic boom, much of the wealth generated by coal stayed in Wales and the industry's scale was only enabled by its position within the British Empire. Wales has been looked down upon and sneered at but the English elite responsible also did the same both to its own workers and cultures throughout the rest of the world.

The exploitation that might seem to be about nation was often really about class. There has never been a deliberate attempt by the English or British state or crown to exterminate the Welsh people or Welsh culture. Modern Wales was kept in the British union not by force but by the votes of the Welsh, the vast majority of whom never showed the slightest inclination to leave. Indeed, wars, religion and Empire created powerful common experiences and emotional bonds between England and Wales. The Welsh used and benefited from the opportunities that being part of the United Kingdom and its Empire afforded them, as much as they sometimes suffered from that same status. They lived and worked amongst the English and were their friends and lovers. The English sometimes laughed at the Welsh but the two also laughed together at other cultures. Medieval Wales was a colony through conquest, but modern Wales was British through choice rather than coercion. Most of the Welsh regarded themselves as partners in Britain, not victims of it.

Yet colonialism is not just about governance. It is also about culture and its legacy can outlast any coercive force which might have created it. Thus the echoes of imperial racism are all around us today, even if European empires are now gone. People may not speak the racist language of their forefathers, but the legacy of those attitudes still exists in continuing inequities and in the very existence of the idea of race, a concept that has no biological reality. In Wales, some maintain that conquest created a mindset of inferiority. The legacy of this is an assumption that Britishness is more important and more powerful, that Wales is too small or too poor to stand alone. It is this, such perspectives maintain, that underpins the Welsh desire to remain in the union. Thus the Britishness to which the Welsh are loyal is a form of false consciousness, something created by the colonialism of hundreds of years before. If this is true, it does not require anyone to have deliberately created or sustained the situation. It is simply a by-product of historical processes. Some call this 'post-colonialism'. Others are happy to stick to the label 'colonialism'.

However, to argue that the Welsh are the victims of the historical legacy of colonialism is to imply that they were (and are) unable to see what was (and is) happening. The historian, Russell Davies, has argued that

> The tendency amongst some historians to blame all the woes of the Welsh on the wiles of the English has given rise to an interpretation of the Welsh in their history as

helpless and hapless, the gormless and guileless victims of a Machiavellian neighbour. Ever since the 'once upon a time', 'long ago', in hopeless skirmishes near streams in the snow when our princes were betrayed, beaten and beheaded, a cycle of abuser-abused-abuser-abused punctuates this nostalgic history. In the melodrama, the Welsh are always the passive victims, the English pernicious victimisers. ... Such views ignore the ability of some Welsh people to fashion a future for themselves.

Blaming England for all the ills, past and present, of Welsh society is to forget how many of the Welsh were willing partners in British industrial, imperialist, cultural and political ventures. To dismiss this as false consciousness is to dismiss the Welsh of the past as stupid, unable to see or understand their own condition. A reluctance to admit to this past owes much to present-day sensibilities. It frees Wales from guilt for the atrocities of the British Empire and from blame for its current economic woes and the fragile state of the Welsh language. In short, it is much easier to blame England for everything that is wrong with Wales.

Denying our own role in our history not only reduces the Welsh of the past to puppets, only able to react to others rather than think for themselves, it also undermines the confidence to act for ourselves in the future. As long as we see ourselves as powerless victims in the past, it will be very difficult to stop seeing ourselves as powerless victims in the present and future. Taking control of the future of Wales means understanding that we had power in the past too. There were certainly times when some of the Welsh were victims of violent oppression but there were times too when the Welsh were complicit in their nation's assimilation into Britain and in the assimilation of many others into Britain's Empire. The lack of national confidence that is so often bemoaned in Wales can be attributed to this present-day perception of national victimhood more than any actual historical oppression.

Although it is precisely what I have just done, there are problems with connecting things that happened in the past to the present day and in seeing this past in terms of oppression and 'us' and 'them'. The Welsh of today are not the same Welsh of the past. Given that anyone living today would have had tens, and maybe hundreds, of thousands of ancestors alive in 1282, the year of the final part of the conquest of Wales, can anyone really claim their ancestors were the victims not the perpetrators? What proportion of someone's ancestors need to be Welsh to say they descend from the oppressed rather than the oppressors? There must be thousands and thousands of Welsh men and women descended in part from settler populations, from English occupation forces, and from economic migrants. Are those people whose Welsh family histories do not stretch back centuries less Welsh than those who are more certain of their family pedigree? Moreover, if to be Welsh today is to claim ancestry with this past, where does that leave those in Wales whose very recent family heritage lies elsewhere? Such questions illustrate how history can hinder residents of present-day Wales in feeling that they belong. Trying to accumulate a score of grievances based on history is thus pointless and also undermining for the very national identity it seeks to bolster. If we go back far enough, there can be few Welsh with no English ancestors. If we go back even further, the terms are meaningless because Wales and England have not always existed. Even when the terms were in existence, they did not always mean the same as they do today. In the twenty-first century, Wales is a defined geographical entity and widely accepted as a nation but in the medieval period being a nation meant being a people more than a place. Today, to understand Wales in ethnic terms is to exclude many of Wales' citizens.

The historian gazing backwards at Wales notices Welshness because it is something familiar to him or her. We thus probe and interrogate it but in doing so perhaps elevate its importance beyond what it meant at the time. The literate elites of past centuries certainly talked about Wales but did it mean anything much to the peasant in the fields, the ironworker at the furnace or the family at the fireside? It's probable that their sense of place was rooted in where they lived, the fields, furnaces and firesides. Some premodern people travelled vast distances but most did not. Their world was a narrow one and thus their loyalty was probably to their community. But that does not mean they had no sense of a wider world. They knew of God and biblical tales. They probably knew of their rulers, although there is no real way to tell. The nineteenth century saw all that change. It brought education, railways and even standardised time, but, even then, nationality was probably not the priority for the people of Wales that it has been for many of the historians of Wales.

History may be complicated but it is one of the central reasons why Welshness survived at all. In the medieval period, the Welsh (or at least the literate ones) had a sense of their antiquity, claiming links back to ancient Greece and the first inhabitants of Britain. But they also had a strong sense of dispossession, lamenting their loss of much of the island to the Saxons. After their eventual conquest, this sense of loss intensified and led to a feeling of being a defeated people. But from the eighteenth century to the present day, the medieval period became key to the survival of Wales because it provided stories of a time when things were different, of a time when the Welsh were self-governing, of when they rose up against their chains of servitude. This was not something that people necessarily thought should be recreated but it did sustain a sense of nationhood. As England and Wales came closer and closer together in political, economic and cultural terms, history offered a sense of consolation, a common inheritance, and a continuing sense of difference. This overlaid internal divisions and offered a sense of being more than just a region or culture. As with so many nations, the exact truths of the national history were irrelevant. It is what people thought had happened that mattered. Indeed, Ernest Renan, a nineteenth-century philosopher, even claimed that getting history wrong is part of being a nation. History has mattered because it has inspired the Welsh to retain their sense of difference and distinctiveness. It gave them stories to understand who they were and to be inspired and angered by. It ensured that the Welsh never started to think of themselves as English. These stories belong to everyone in Wales today, regardless of their personal heritage. They are about a place and a culture, not ancestry, race or DNA.

History may have sustained Welsh identity but what it should mean for the present is open to interpretation. There are those who think the political future of the United Kingdom should be based on lessons from its past, whether they see that history in terms of English colonialism or shared ventures. There are those who are angry about things that happened, or things they think that happened. History can thus raise awkward questions or possibilities for the present and future. At its most extreme, tales of violence from the past might encourage violence in the present. In 1913, one school history book told readers:

> If you and I had fought by the side of Llewelyn the Last, doubtless we should have felt very bitter, when we saw our friends killed, our farms taken from us, and our families cruelly treated by a king who could not excuse himself by saying that he was bringing us the blessings of a better civilisation.
>
> But it is not justifiable for the Welsh to feel bitter against the English now. The conditions are quite changed. The English government is no longer free to oppress a Welshman, to injure his friends, or treat his family cruelly. The law protects a Welshman from a bad Englishman in exactly the same way as it protects an Englishman from a bad Welshman. In law, Welshmen and Englishmen are absolutely equal.
>
> Wales is, we say, united with England; and union is strength.

This book was trying to reconcile the past and present and to draw lessons from history. Yet its reading of what those lessons were was based more on its understanding of the present. The same book also told readers that Glyndŵr's rebellion took place in very different circumstances because then individuals had no power and thus had to resort to violence, whereas now power lay with the people through an elected Parliament. The past is always read through the prism of the present and thus the present reads into it whatever suits it. The reality is that there are no clear lessons from the past, only tantalising hints to be plundered and moulded to suit pre-existing political beliefs. Every society needs to know its past but it also needs to be wary of basing its future on that past.

I hope that this book does not just speak to Wales. It is in the English conquest of Wales that the origins of a multinational and multicultural British state lie. If England wants to understand itself better, it would do well to look at its first colony. Here lie the origins of its confusion, of why it has been left behind by devolution, of why it struggles to understand the difference between Englishness and Britishness. It has forgotten what its early kings knew, that the places to its west and north were different. It has also forgotten that the response of those kings was to think England was the most important component of this island, with a natural right to superiority over the other inhabitants. What was once conscious has become unconscious. Just as the source of Britain's relative wealth lies in its imperial past, the inequalities within Britain lie deep in its history too. Britain was never the coming together of equals that the voluntary union of

England and Scotland has fooled people into thinking. Those that look back further realise that Britain was made by conquest. Perhaps then it is not surprising that Britain went on to think it had a right to conquer much of the rest of the world. The history of Wales does not offer answers to England's problems, but it does help an understanding of them.

Whatever happened in the past and whatever happens in the future, Wales will continue to be defined by its relationship with England. The island is just too small and England too big for anything else ever to be true. This book thus explores the history of that relationship between Wales and England and of what it has meant to be Welsh. The first section explores how the very idea of Wales was created by the relationships of its peoples with the Anglo-Saxons and the kingdom of England they formed. It looks at how the gradual conquest of Wales cemented that idea of Wales and how colonisation intensified it. The second section investigates how political assimilation liberated the Welsh from colonisation and also drove a wider process of cultural and economic assimilation. The coming together of political, cultural and economic forces saw Wales lose some of its distinctiveness. There was never a deliberate and sustained English project to make this happen but assimilation happened all the same, masking the inequalities that existed within the British union. The third section shows how assimilation had not destroyed Welsh identity. It underwent a revival and refashioning in the nineteenth century, before being undermined by mid twentieth-century economic collapse and rebuilding. Fears that Wales was being marginalised and in peril created new efforts to recreate Wales again. The nation gradually gained official rights and recognition and its first ever degree of democratic national self-government. Yet the realities and practicalities of politics, economics and culture meant Wales remained tied to England.

I

Conquest

The word nation comes from the Latin 'natio', meaning a group of people. It did not refer to a geographic space. The idea of a people sharing enough to become a community or group is strongest when they meet those who are different. This was how the very idea of Wales came about. It was not until the people we now call the Welsh lost parts of the island of Britain to Germanic settlers and their descendants that the idea of Wales developed. At first, they continued to call themselves the Britons and feel the whole island belonged to them, wherever they lived within it. But, gradually, the people pushed into the margins of their island became removed from each other and accepted the new political reality, especially after the Normans took over England in 1066 and began expanding its political limits. Those living in one western peninsula came to accept that the Cymry, their fellow countrymen, were those in the same place as them rather than in Cornwall, Brittany, and northern England. When they wrote the name of the country in Latin, they even began to use the name the inhabitants of England had given them: Wallia, a term derived from the English word for foreigner.

Yet medieval Wales remained divided, a collection of kingdoms that were at war with each other as much as with those to the east in England. Paradoxically, conquest overcame this. The first Norman incursions into Wales sharpened the sense the Welsh had of being different from those to the east. It also encouraged the native rulers to try to develop a Welsh state capable of withstanding the external threat. This failed but the final stage of its conquest brought a new unity to Wales through ending its different kingdoms and giving the Welsh a stronger common identity through persecution and defeat. Thus, in some ways, it was England that first made Wales and then bolstered this new nation by conquering it.

Of course, had Wales not been conquered, Welsh identity might perhaps have strengthened anyway. After all, the medieval period saw a process of building political states based on national communities across Europe and two princes of Gwynedd had already tried to establish a Welsh state in the thirteenth century. But not all peoples with a strong common identity become nations. Here it is worth considering what happened to Cumbria. Like Wales, it was not settled by the Anglo-Saxons and continued to speak a Brythonic (Celtic) language. Like Wales, it was annexed by a neighbour, the Scots in the early eleventh century. But, at the end of that century, it was divided between Scotland and England and its sense of identity faded away.

Wales avoided this fate. One reason was geography. The mountains cut Wales off, limiting its demographic, cultural and linguistic integration with first the Saxons and then the Normans. A second reason was that neither the English Crown nor the individual Norman barons who carried out the first stages of conquest ever tried to obliterate Welsh identity or fully assimilate the country into

16

England. Thus, having unintentionally made Wales, England did not intentionally try to unmake it either. Instead, throughout the medieval period, Wales was treated with a curious mix of disdain, disinterest, and colonial oppression.

Wales before the Normans

When the Romans arrived in what we now call Wales they thought the land was inhabited by four different tribes: Deceangli on the north coast, Ordovices in the mountains, Silures in the south east and Demetae in the west. Whether these tribes existed in any coherent form is a different matter but that was how the Romans interpreted the peoples they found. Today, we often think of them, and the rest of the inhabitants of Britain, as Celtic. However, this was a Roman term used to describe different peoples across much of Europe and they never applied it to Britain. Despite a common material culture, there was no political unity across either Wales or Britain at this time. DNA evidence suggests that the ancient people of north and south Wales were genetically distinct not just to people in England but to one another too. It is not even clear that the whole of Britain spoke the Brythonic languages that evolved into Welsh, Gaelic and Gallic. The idea of pre-Roman Celtic British culture is a romantic one but it masks diversity and disunity.

Whoever they were, at some point nearly two thousand years ago, the residents of Britain were conquered by the Romans. It was not a peaceful conquest and in Wales it culminated in an attack on Anglesey, where the invaders massacred an army of frenzied druids, women and others who believed in covering their altars with the blood of their captives and using the entrails to speak to the gods. Or at least that is what the Roman writer Tacitus recorded. Not for the last time, the people of Wales were subject to some vicious propaganda from outsiders who thought them barbarians. Perhaps it was not unsurprising then some of them became Romanised, speaking Latin, wearing togas, drinking wine and living in villas. A conquered people, or at least members of its elite, allied itself to the might of an empire for the prestige, power and perhaps peace that it offered. Again, this would not be the last time.

But this is to look backwards from the Wales of today. For the four hundred-odd years the Romans were there, Wales was just the western peninsula of the island they called Britain. Yet the Roman conquest did leave a mark that can still be seen in Wales today. The Welsh language includes words from Latin such as llyfr, pont and ystafell. Welsh geography is marked by the places where the Romans decided to build forts and towns. Most importantly, the end of their rule of Britain left a vacuum into which stepped groups that were to help make Wales itself. Collectively they have become known as the Anglo-Saxons. Quite when or why they came is not clear. It may be that many were already living in eastern Britain before the Romans left, but gradually, over maybe a couple of hundred years, they spread west and north across England and their language and culture became implanted in those places. Whether this owed more to violence, mass migration or a cultural transformation of the existing population is impossible to know. Later writers told tales of great battles and slaughter, and of a man called Arthur who led the native resistance. Archaeology and DNA evidence suggests something less violent, a great intermingling of peoples. However, the language of England is clear evidence of which culture eventually came out on top.

The Anglo-Saxons did not make it to the Welsh peninsula in any great numbers and this created a new cultural and linguistic difference between the lands we now call Wales and England. This difference was given a physical marker in the eighth century when the king of Mercia, one of the kingdoms the Anglo-Saxons formed, had a dyke built to protect his land from raiders to the west. It was probably based on existing dykes and was more than just a defensive structure: the extensive resources needed to build Offa's Dyke made it a statement of power. Although it did not run the entire length of the border, it, together with the Severn in the south, did symbolically shut off the Britons to the west, in effect creating the place that came to be called Wales and cementing the idea that the people there were different. This gave them a tentative unity that had not existed before. A sense of difference to the peoples to the east, and the idea of a border with these peoples, consequently forged a link between the north and south of Wales that simply had not been there before.

However, beneath the symbolism, lived realities were more fluid. There were British communities to the east of Offa's Dyke and increasingly there were Saxon ones to its west. The border was a crossing point as much as a barrier and communities intermingled and interacted. Rare surviving tenth-century legal documents suggest the Welsh and Anglo-Saxons living near each other learned to accommodate and treat the other as equals. They developed mechanisms that drew on the laws of both cultures to resolve differences that might cause bloodshed and to protect mutual interests from outsiders. One example of the complexity of the border was Archenfield. It was to the west of the river Wye, then regarded as the border, but, at some point, it came under the control of Mercia. However, it remained in the diocese of Llandaf, the English system of local governance was not imposed on it and its inhabitants continued to speak what we now call Welsh. It also still used Welsh law but with some modifications that facilitated payments to the Mercian crown.

Such hybrid areas might indicate that there was no clear border but the idea of the Welsh and Anglo-Saxons as distinct peoples with distinct territories remained powerful. The fuzzy boundaries do not change how the Anglo-Saxons essentially made Wales, by not conquering the land and thus creating a cultural division within southern Britain. They even gave the Britons a new name, *Wealas* or *Walas*, a term that might be best translated as foreign or strange. In time, this term would come to be used for the Welsh only. The Anglo-Saxons thus not only in essence created a place called Wales, they named it too. Moreover, the Anglo-Saxon control of much of southern Britain was to shape the people who would become the Welsh in one other fundamental way. It left them with a sense of having been dispossessed from their rightful control over the island and a mythology that one day someone, a new Arthur, would lead them back to their inheritance.

Yet the Welsh were far from a united people, let alone

anything we might call a political unit. Although the people shared a common language and sense of ancestry, Wales was a complex mix of minor kingdoms competing for power, land and influence. Their exact nature is lost to history, as is whether they felt any common bond beyond not being Saxon. But some of their names at least are familiar to us. In the northwest was Gwynedd, in the southwest was Dyfed, in the east was Brycheiniog, and in the southeast was Glywysing. Their boundaries and shape were not fixed and shifted with the incessant armed conflicts and disputes brought about by the Welsh custom of dividing land and lordship inheritances between all sons rather than just everything going to the eldest. Nor were they exclusively Welsh. Archaeology and historic placenames such as Fishguard, Haverford, Milford Haven, Swansea and Anglesey suggest that there were Irish, English and Scandinavian settlers along the Welsh coast. By the eleventh century, the Welsh kingdoms had evolved into Gwynedd, Powys, Morgannwg and Deheubarth. Viking raids and incessant internal pillage, plunder and political turmoil were not conducive to trade or urban life and Wales remained relatively poor and without any major urban centre. In contrast, through trade and politics, the Anglo-Saxon kingdom of Wessex became a powerful military and economic unit. Gradually, it overcame both the Vikings and other English kingdoms and formed a new Kingdom of England.

The gradual unification of England – which began in the ninth century under Alfred in response to the external Viking threat – had profound significance for the people of the land of Wales. It cemented their sense of cultural difference to those to the east and made the dreams of a recovery of control over Britain unlikely. But both the Welsh and English were Christian and that gave them something in common in the face of raids by pagan Norsemen. Moreover, even before English unification, the Anglo-Saxon rulers were beginning to believe themselves as having a claim of sorts on the land of Wales. None tried to conquer Wales but by the tenth century the most powerful Anglo-Saxon rulers regarded themselves as some sort of British head king and they expected the Welsh to acknowledge this hierarchy. In 927, Hywel Dda, despite ruling most of Wales outside the south-east, submitted to Aethelstan, king of Wessex, acknowledging him as his overlord. This won him a new ally against both his Welsh rivals and the external Viking threat that plagued the Welsh coast. Indeed, throughout the medieval period, English influence over Wales would owe much to it being invited by Welsh rulers seeking an advantage over their compatriots.

It was through marriage and war that Hywel Dda had come to rule all Wales except for Morgannwg. But this was a rare moment of relative political unity for Wales. A century later, Gruffudd ap Llywelyn, King of Gwynedd, took Deheubarth and then Morgannwg through force, killing those who opposed him and those who might. From 1055 until 1063, he ruled all Wales. These eight years represent the only time Wales can really claim to have been one independent nation. But it was achieved by brutality and fear and this was perhaps why it was someone Welsh who killed him in 1063 and sent his head to the English king. After his death, Wales fractured again and the Welsh returned to being a people spread across four kingdoms rather than a political entity. Moreover, the whole idea of Wales as a nation or kingdom remained invisible. This was because, despite the way their sense of difference to England probably gave them some feeling of unity, the Welsh seemed to continue to think of themselves as Britons with a cultural inheritance and identity based, not upon the western peninsula where they lived, but on the whole island.

The first stages of the conquest of Wales and the Welsh

In 1093, Rhys ap Tewdwr, the King of Deheubarth, was killed. The murder of a Welsh leader was not unusual in what was often a bloody and brutal world but this time the act was blamed on the Normans, the aristocratic group from France who had seized control of the English crown in 1066 and of England itself in the years that followed. The Battle of Hastings precipitated not just the invasion of England but of parts of Wales too. Norman lords grabbed land across the whole of south Wales and in pockets of the north. This was not an organised or a crown-sponsored conquest but rather the actions of individual barons with a significant technological edge. To protect their conquests, they built castles, with one at Chepstow being started as early as 1067. These structures began as simple wooden fortifications on high earthen mounds or natural peaks, designed to be held by small numbers. But they gradually turned into large stone structures which stamped Norman authority on the landscape and reminded the natives of who was in charge and just how powerful they were. Castles were not the only advantage the Normans had. Wales had little iron and thus nothing like the chainmail and swords of the Normans, who were also able to produce weapons in greater quantities thanks to their more advanced economy. The invaders were more experienced and better trained, with their aristocracy raised in a deeply militarised culture and taught to fight from an early age. Their cavalry gave them movement and speed while also enabling devastating charges. This was of less use in the uplands and mountains but it was central to how quickly lowland Wales fell to the new force.

The Normans expanded into Wales because they sought more land and power. The invasion of England had been an opportunity for individuals to gain territories and fortunes and including Wales in their ambitions was probably just an extension of this. But there was also a racial dimension to their ambitions. The Normans seem to have regarded the Welsh as lazy, promiscuous and brutal warlike barbarians who were in need of civilising. One mid twelfth-century writer even described them as 'bestial'. These differences were believed to be inherent racial characteristics and thus the will of God. This provided a divine justification for Norman expansion into Welsh lands and the crushing of Welsh independence. Such political expediency does not mean these were not genuine beliefs. The Normans, like the English after them, fixated on the differences rather the similarities. They saw in Wales a world less structured and wilder than their own. Wales was more mountainous and forested; it was colder and wetter and lacking in villages, towns, and even coinage and agricultural fields. The people were strange in tongue, dress and custom. Marriage between first cousins was allowed and both concubines and illegitimate children had legal status. The Normans were also horrified at Welsh habits in war. They expected prisoners of rank to be treated with respect, whereas the Welsh sometimes killed or mutilated them. In addition, the Welsh sometimes made slaves of prisoners of no rank and sold them. Again, this seemed barbaric to the Normans. Such thinking added a form of cultural imperialism to that of military might and was just as important in asserting and legitimising power and authority over the Welsh.

By the early twelfth century, most of south Wales, including all the richest agricultural lands, was under Norman control. This divided Wales into two. Latin writers called the part that remained under native rule, Pura Wallia (Welsh Wales), whereas the occupied section became known as Marchia Walliae (the March of Wales). The lords that controlled the March were hugely powerful in their own right and liked to think they were beyond the command of the King. They introduced new Norman notions of law and order which were radically different to Welsh concepts of liability. When an individual rebelled or broke the law, the Welsh had traditionally punished his whole community by seeking livestock compensation from all. The Marcher Lords, in contrast, held an individual responsible, taking his land and sometimes his life. This ripped apart tradition and communities and destabilised native Welsh society. Even the Welsh church suffered. Some of its churches were re-dedicated from Welsh saints to ones with which the Normans were familiar. The authority of the Welsh church was further challenged by the new Norman overlords introducing monasteries, usually populated by monks from outside Wales. With their taxes and control over surrounding land and peoples, these were as much instruments of conquest and subjugation as any castle.

A Welsh priest, Rhigyfarch, wrote of the Norman conquest of south Wales in the late eleventh century:

> The people and the priest are despised, by the word, heart and deeds of the Frenchmen. They burden us with tribute and consume our possessions. One of them, however lowly, shakes a hundred natives, with his command and terrifies them with his look. Alas, our fall, alas the deep grief.

But the conquest of the March was not a straightforward process. There were constant revolts and raids caused by the desire of Welsh rulers to regain their own power and by what another Welsh chronicler called 'the unbearable tyranny, injustice, oppression and violence of the French'. Thus while some parts of Wales were always firmly in Norman hands, others such as Builth, had chequered histories with control swinging back and forth between the Welsh and the conquerors. Nor was it just men who felt the injustice, despite the fact that Welsh law prohibited women from owning land. In 1136, with her husband, a prince of Deheubarth, away, Gwenllian ferch Gruffydd led an army to defend his lands against Norman attempts to put down a growing uprising. She was captured in battle and beheaded. The Normans put such revolts down to the Welsh love of war. Gerald of Wales, a monk who claimed both Welsh and Norman ancestry, even wrote that the Welsh were a people happy to die in battle but who thought it a disgrace to die in bed. Whether this was true or not, the long and drawn out conquest of the Welsh had begun and it turned much of Wales into a warzone plagued by raiding and guerrilla fighting. As a result, there were around four hundred castles across Wales by 1215.

Some today like to interpret as a sign of Welsh national virility how long it took the Normans to suppress Wales. The reality was that the English kings and barons were just not that interested in this periphery to their lands. It was the politics of England and France that mattered to them and thus they were usually too preoccupied to throw their weight at Wales, especially since its richest lowlands were now taken. Norman expansion into Wales stuttered to an almost stop as England descended into civil war during the troubled reign of King Stephen. Such moments, like the later political chaos of King John's reign, allowed the Welsh to regroup and push back, but these were only temporary reprieves. It was no coincidence that when an English king properly turned his attention to conquering the Welsh in the late thirteenth century, the English crown's lands in France were all but gone.

Once Welsh land was taken, there was no real attempt to make it part of England in any legal or administrative sense. Instead it became a sort of buffer zone between native-controlled Wales and England. The Marcher lords did not introduce shires and made no systematic attempt to impose other structures of English governance. Unlike in northern England, the Normans conquered rather than assimilated the March and in the longer term this too helped Welsh identity survive. There were, however, attempts to develop and civilise the March. They imported English peasants to live and farm lands around their castles, possibly moving the native population to make way for them. There were also new immigrant towns around some castles which, despite having some Welsh inhabitants, became islands of the English language in a sea of Welsh-speaking countryside. The scale of Anglo-Norman influence on settlement patterns and the population is evident in the fact that are still around three hundred and fifty place names ending in the classic English form of -ton in what was the March. Thus something resembling parallel societies emerged. There were districts, sometimes known as Englishries and usually on lowland, based around English settlers and using English feudal and legal systems. But near them remained traditional Welsh social structures using Welsh laws. The divisions were as much economic as ethnic and not all were based on the implantation of settlers. In the Radnor Englishry, for example, just half of taxable people in the late thirteenth century had English names. In such Englishries, taxes were paid in cash or labour, whereas in the Welsh areas of the March dues were paid in goods.

South Pembrokeshire also witnessed demographic change. In the early twelfth century, Henry I invited Flemish immigrants, who were renowned as hardy colonisers, to settle and establish a cloth trade. This took place alongside English immigration and place names again show just how extensive the anglicisation of the area was. What happened to the Welsh of south Pembrokeshire is not clear. There is some suggestion in medieval Welsh writings of them being driven away by the colonists but it may be that some assimilated with the newcomers, with such peaceful co-operation not deemed newsworthy by Welsh medieval chroniclers. However, modern DNA analysis shows that parts of the modern population of south Pembrokeshire have a different genetic makeup from those in the north of the county. This does suggest that the native medieval population was replaced rather than assimilated. There was also some ongoing bitterness about the English and Flemish presence, suggesting that something violent had happened. Fighting and raiding was not uncommon and in 1134 the contemporary writer Orderic Vitalis had claimed the Flemish 'butchered' the Welsh 'like dogs, without any regard for humanity whenever they could track them out in the woods and caves in which they lurked'. Nearly a century later, Llywelyn ap Iorwerth, Prince of Gwynedd, attacked the area, slaughtering the Flemish, an example of how ethnic violence could linger and breed yet more violence.

The question of ethnicity in this period is complicated by the fact that this first stage of the conquest of Wales was led by Norman rather than English lords. Like the King, they spoke French and regarded their English lands in the same light as their Welsh and Irish ones, the fruits of conquest. Indeed, England was not itself a state. First, it was part of what essentially was a Norman empire and then, from the time of Henry II (1154-89), an empire that included vast swathes of France. Wales was on the edge of both but the eyes of England's rulers were on their borders with the French king, a far more dangerous threat than anyone in Wales.

The impact of Norman incursions on Welsh thinking was significant. The remaining Welsh leaders looked for new titles since their claims to kingship seemed weak in the face of Norman power. Calling themselves lords or princes was less open to dispute. This did not mean they were lowering their ambitions. The term 'prince' and its Welsh form *tywysog* both had a much wider meaning than the son of a king and they signified a leader or ruler. Conquest also had a profound impact on conceptions of national and ethnic identity. Like the Anglo-Saxon threat before it, the Norman conquest strengthened Welsh identity. The sense and awareness of a common Welsh history, language and law were sharpened now they were under clear threat. That there was a single Welsh law was credited to Hywel Dda, the tenth-century king of Deheubarth. Quite how it came about is not clear but its existence was remarkable given how politically divided Wales had been. Now that English law was encroaching into Wales, Welsh law became a cornerstone of Welsh consciousness and difference. Yet Welsh identity was much more than a matter of politics and symbolism. Just as the Normans perceived the Welsh as a distinct people so too did the Welsh think of themselves in such a way. Today, we think of national and racial differences as cultural but in the medieval world, they were regarded as natural and ordained categories created by God. This meant that to medieval eyes the Welsh remained Welsh wherever they went and those who came to Wales also retained their own racial identity. Thus, both the Welsh and Normans recognised Welsh, English, French and Flemish peoples within Wales.

The heightened sense of Welsh identity was evident in how the Welsh stopped thinking of themselves as the Britons. The term *Cymry* had been sometimes employed to refer to the Britons across the island before the Norman conquest but at the start of the twelfth century it began to displace Welsh-language references to the Welsh as the Britons and it became clearly focussed on the people of Wales rather than a wider population. This change in mindset was visible in Latin writings too. The old English term *'Wealas'* may have once been derogatory but it was appropriated by the Welsh and increasingly used by Welsh clerics from the twelfth century to refer both to the parts of Wales remaining under native rule and the wider area that included the March. This distinguished the Welsh from other British peoples and was perhaps also employed because there was a desire to use a term that the English understood. Whatever the reasoning it was an important step in the transformation of the Welsh into a nation because it recognised that Wales was a place rather than just a people. Some today still see the terms Wales and Welsh as oppressive, symbols of anglicisation or a nation's marginalisation within the British Isles. But what was once an Anglo-Saxon term of difference, and perhaps even abuse, was appropriated by the medieval Welsh elite and used to declare their sense of place and identity.

Yet, for all the existence of an ethnic Welsh people with a common law, culture and history, Wales remained fractious and fragmented in political terms. This was partly a matter of geography in a mountainous country difficult to travail. But the lack of unity was political and cultural too. In the parts of the land beyond Norman control, power and borders ebbed and flowed between and within the kingdoms of Deheubarth, Powys and Gwynedd. Personality, opportunism and brute force shaped realities. Under Welsh law, on a ruler's death, his land was divided up between all sons, legitimate and illegitimate. This was a recipe for an unstable political climate. Deheubarth, for example, fractured after Lord Rhys' fifteen sons set about themselves after his death in 1197. Battles between the Welsh were bloody and brutal, with murder and recriminations common and nothing like the code of conduct which governed how the Normans treated other nobles. Family and rivals were killed, blinded, mutilated or castrated. There was little attempt to unite in the face of the Norman intrusions. At first, the Marcher lords were simply another player in this brutal political game. Thus, rather than come together against this foe, Welsh rulers made alliances and marriages with the Normans to gain advantage over their rival compatriots. Lord Rhys, for example, may have been probably the most powerful native ruler the south had ever known but he worked closely with the Crown and even sent a thousand men to fight for Henry II in France in 1174. Women could play their part in these alliances too and were not always mere pawns in a political world centred on men. Those married to Normans could actively help uphold and strengthen the alliances with their Welsh families, whilst Norman women married to Welsh men supported and promoted their husband's power. One notable example was Nest, the daughter of an eleventh-century king of Deheubarth. She was married to the Norman castellan of Pembroke and protected his interests against her Welsh cousin who was waging war against him and ended up abducting and perhaps raping her. Her personality and beauty appears to have given her some power and she ensured her brother was given refuge at Pembroke despite his violent attempts to recover control of Deheubarth. The complex family dynamics at play illustrate how it was not simply through force that the Normans established a place in Wales. Marriages created loyalties that crossed national boundaries and tied Welsh and Norman families together.

The rise and fall of Gwynedd

In the thirteenth century, Gwynedd emerged as the most powerful of the Welsh kingdoms. This was to provide the basis of another major shift in how Wales was seen. The supremacy of Gwynedd over the rest of native-controlled Wales was helped by how it was both open and closed to the world. Its mountains and westerly position protected it from Norman advances. Yet its people travelled, gaining experience of war, the law and trade from other places. Its leadership was willing to learn from England and copied their stone castles, weapons, taxes and urban charters. The ruler that first pushed Gwynedd forward was Llywelyn ap Iorweth (1173-1240), who was to become known as Llywelyn Fawr (the Great). Although he took advantage of political turmoil in England under King John, more often than not he tried to ally himself with rather than against England. He acknowledged the Crown's overlordship, served with John's army in Scotland, and married the King's illegitimate daughter, Joan. This was pragmatic politics since it stopped the

Crown either backing his rivals or intervening militarily to stop his growing power within Wales. Helped by his English alliance, he claimed and secured overlordship over the other Welsh native rulers, although he did not adopt the title Prince of Wales nor make direct claims on Welsh land in the March. To protect his territorial and political gains, he adopted the English custom of passing everything to one legitimate son rather than seeing his power and land divided between his male offspring.

It did not work. After his death, Llywelyn's two sons fought over their inheritance and his advances towards a unified Wales collapsed. But they were revived by his grandson, Llywelyn ap Gruffudd. After first defeating his brothers, he went further than his grandfather in trying to forge a political Wales. Taking advantage of the problems of the English King Henry III, he declared himself Prince of Wales. This title was both an effort to assert power over the other native Welsh rulers and to establish a Welsh state with its own laws, customs and political structure, albeit one that recognised the reality that the March was already lost. This vision, even if based on a reduced Wales, showed that rather than being crushed by political realities, national consciousness and political ambitions had actually been strengthened. There is an irony here in the present-day objections to the idea of Wales as a principality on the grounds that it signals Wales' subjugation. For Llywelyn, being Prince of Wales was a signal of Welsh independence and something to build a state around. It was also these ambitions that made the term Wales or Wallia so important. Britain was too ambiguous and removed from political realities, whereas Wallia was defined and understood by the English. However, his principality probably lacked any real coherence and was more a loose alliance of different Welsh areas pulled together by the personal and military force of Llywelyn and Gwynedd. Moreover, whether it was welcomed by the ordinary people living within it is disputable. Given that Gwynedd imposed new taxes on them, it might even be said that these steps towards a Welsh state were actually rather regressive for the masses. They also made Wales more vulnerable. A decentralised and disparate mix of competing territories was harder to conquer completely than a single political entity. The new power of Gwynedd meant that if it fell so too would the whole of independent Wales.

In 1267, the English crown through the Treaty of Montgomery recognised Llywelyn as Prince of Wales with a right to accept homage from other Welsh native nobles. This made Llywelyn the first and last recognised native Prince of Wales. But the fact that the recognition of the English crown was needed illustrated the illusory nature of Welsh independence. Worse, Llywelyn had to pay twenty-five thousand marks for the privilege of being acknowledged as Prince. At this time, his annual income may have been around five thousand marks and thus it represented an exorbitant cost. The financial burden was to be paid in instalments, but it was to cause Llywelyn ongoing problems and it was another marker of the limits of Gwynedd and Wales' independence and of how far its leaders were willing to go to secure English recognition. Moreover, the contradiction of an independent ruler who was still subject to the overlordship of a foreign king was bound to cause tension in the future if the crown ever saw its position as anything more than symbolic. The English king may not have had the title of King of Britain but that was what in effect he was becoming.

By this time, the name of the people against whom the Welsh were defining themselves against had changed. The Norman Conquest transformed the language of power in England and the Marcher lords who began the conquest of Wales spoke French not English. But English remained the language of the people of England and Norman lords had English servants, officials and probably even wet nurses. Gradually, over a few generations or more, the Norman aristocracy began to speak English and even think of themselves as English. The loss of the King of England's continental lands in the early thirteenth century accelerated that process because it meant the crown no longer had an empire in France to be distracted by. In 1272, England even gained its first king since 1066 to bear an English name. He was called Edward and he was to have a profound impact on the course of Welsh history.

By then Llywelyn was already facing significant problems, despite or perhaps because of his new title. The Treaty of Montgomery had been rather vague as to how far the Principality and his power extended, and there were inevitable tensions along its ill-defined borders. Llywelyn thought he was owed homage by the remaining Welsh lords within Glamorgan, which was in the March rather than within his Principality. The Earl of Gloucester, however, felt he was the overlord of that area and began work on a castle at Caerphilly to reaffirm his position. Llywelyn took this as a threat and unsuccessfully tried to destroy it in 1270. Further tensions emerged when Llywelyn began to build a market and castle at Dolforwyn (Powys) in 1273. Feeling this area was under his jurisdiction, a marcher lord ordered him to stop but he refused, claiming his right to build castles on his own land. In essence, his Principality was too new for there to be established custom over how the border should be managed and where he had the right to exert his authority and where he did not. But even within the Principality, there was resentment of Llywelyn's new power on the part of the other Welsh leaders expected to do him homage and pay him taxes. The political project of a Welsh state was seen as a mask for Gwynedd power rather than Welsh independence from England and it seems to have won little enthusiasm in the kingdoms of Powys and Deheubarth. Indeed, such was Llywelyn's unpopularity as Prince of Wales that even his brother Dafydd plotted to kill him.

Amidst these tensions, Llywelyn made significant political mistakes. He aggravated the Crown by trying to marry Eleanor de Montfort, who was the King's cousin but also the daughter of a powerful but now dead rebel named Simon de Montfort. He refused to pay what he owed the King under the Treaty of Montgomery and repeatedly failed to obey summons to do homage to Edward. The King eventually lost patience and invaded north Wales in 1276-7 with a substantial army. He found ready allies in Wales, cut off Anglesey, the key source of grain for Gwynedd, with his navy, and won a crushing military victory. The resulting Treaty of Aberconwy saw Llywelyn forced to give up land and huge sums of money, and it led to the establishment of large new English castles at Aberystwyth, Builth, Flint and Rhuddlan. The building of what today is sometimes called the iron ring of castles had begun and what remained of Welsh independence was becoming encircled. Llywelyn did get to keep his title but only for his lifetime, a sign that Edward wanted to end Welsh independence. Nonetheless, the King had reacted to events rather than led them. But he also seemed determined to ensure that no one was in any doubt where power lay. In 1278, he allowed Llywelyn to marry Eleanor de Montfort and even paid for the wedding feast. This tied the ruling houses of Wales and England together, but it was Edward who decided on the date and location of the wedding.

The new arrangements were not harmonious. New taxes and the abuses of local crown officials in administering them led to a Welsh rebellion in 1282, this time led by Llywelyn's brother, who had fought with the crown in 1276-77. The scale of the local injustices meant that other Welsh leaders joined him, despite their resentment of Gwynedd. Llywelyn did not incite the new rebellion but he had his own problems and grievances. The King had ruled against him in a dispute over whose jurisdiction some land in the upper Severn valley fell and his wife had died in childbirth. In reality, he probably had little choice but to act if he wanted to maintain his position as leader of the native Welsh. The rebellion caused Edward to invade again. The Archbishop of Canterbury tried to mediate a settlement. There was even an offer from Edward of an English earldom for the Welsh prince but he replied that the people of Snowdonia were 'unwilling to do homage to a stranger with whose language, customs and laws they are unfamiliar. For if that were to happen they might be made captive forever and be treated cruelly'. This was inspiring and patriotic talk but it clearly went against the established tradition of English overlordship that he himself had recognised and followed.

Whatever the reason, by confronting rather than co-operating with England, Llywelyn overplayed his hand and condemned what was left of a free Wales. Edward's tolerance was broken and he sought a swift end to the last of Welsh independence. In the face of another invasion by overwhelming English force, Llywelyn headed south for reasons that are unclear, only somehow to be separated from his men and killed in a chance encounter or ambush near Builth Wells. What happened is not certain, but Llywelyn's death essentially marked the end of the last of Welsh independence. His head was sent to London, where it was stuck on a spike at the gate of the Tower of London, and crowned with ivy, a symbol of outlawry. It was said to be still there fifteen years later.

Llywelyn's brother Dafydd fought on but the heat and base of support for the fight vanished. Six months later, Dafydd was captured and became the first person to be hung, drawn and quartered. This was a shocking punishment given the English Crown's tradition of treating high-born prisoners relatively well. Perhaps it was personal since the king knew Dafydd well and had been supported by him in the 1276-77 invasion. But it left no doubt as to who had won and would have been long remembered by any future potential rebels. The King also set about removing anyone on whom a future rebellion might centre. Dafydd's sons, Llywelyn's nephews, spent the rest of their lives imprisoned at an English castle, with one even condemned for a time to sleep in a cage. Llywelyn's daughter Gwenllian was sent to an English monastery where she spent her whole life, unlikely, even, to have been able to speak Welsh.

In the eyes of the English Crown, conquest brought an end to the idea of Wales as a separate political unit. This was clear in the 1284 Statute of Wales which declared that Pura Wallia (i.e. native-run Wales rather than the March) and its people had been 'annexed and united to the crown of the said kingdom as part of the said body'. To demonstrate this, the regalia and holy relics of the Gwynedd princes, including a supposed fragment of Jesus' cross, were moved to the shrine of Edward the Confessor at Westminster, a symbolic gesture to show that English royalty had subsumed Welsh royalty. Another symbolic act was the naming of the King's son, born at Caernarfon in 1301, as Prince of Wales. He and his descendants were given control of the land which had been held by the dynasties that had rebelled, thus making the Crown the largest landowner in Wales. It was perhaps little wonder then that the bards of Wales saw the fall of Gwynedd and its allies as cataclysmic, a kind of judgment day on the Welsh. One simply asked if it was the end of the world. A chronicler declared 'And then all Wales was cast to the ground'. It is not always the winners who write history.

A conquered people

The English saw their victory as some sort of moral justice and felt they were bringing the benefits of civilisation to the remaining Welsh not previously under their rule. This meant there was no attempt to wring every drop out of Wales and the Welsh for English benefit. Those who had rebelled from the Welsh royal dynasties beyond Gwynedd did lose their lands and in some cases their freedom. Yet there was no complete destruction of the upper echelons of Welsh society. There must also have been some Welsh who welcomed the end of the conflict since wars always bring death, famine and misery. Moreover, there had actually been a fair few Welsh who had fought on the English side.

Nor was there any attempt to destroy the idea of Wales as a place apart. The March remained untouched, the Principality retained its title and post-conquest it was referred to in English legal documents as a 'land', an acknowledgement that it was different even if it was no longer a distinct political unit. Indeed, Wales' strangeness was enhanced not eradicated as conquest left Wales a patchwork of royal lands, a semi-autonomous March under the governance of its own lords, and parts of Powys still in the hands of natives who had been loyal to the crown during the war of 1282-83. (Indeed, areas in Powys can claim to be the only part of Wales never conquered.) Welsh law was not abolished, at least not in its entirety. Those laws that offended English religious sensibility were superseded and thus came to an end the Welsh tradition of illegitimate sons inheriting. Criminal Welsh law went too because it saw theft and even violence as a matter between two parties that could be dealt with by paying compensation, whereas English law saw it as breaking the king's peace and thus the king's power. There were even Welsh beneficiaries of these changes. Most notably, under the English laws introduced, women were now allowed to own and inherit land, whereas under Welsh law they had not been allowed to own land at all. In a way, however, this just formalised something that already been happening in practice. English women who married into Welsh noble families had already pushed for their English rights to count in Wales and thus to be allowed to own land on their husband's death. Some Welsh noble women had done the same, illustrating the influence England had on Welsh society even before conquest and how aspects of the drive for assimilation had come from within Wales.

Not only was Welsh identity not stamped out but there were some attempts to win it over to the new political reality. Welsh churches were compensated for damages they suffered during the war. Welsh families were denied access to the most important administrative roles but most local official posts remained in Welsh hands. Edward I, like the rulers of Rome before him and the British Empire afterwards, knew that keeping some locals onside was key to governance. The Crown was quite happy to reward Welsh figures who helped uphold the new arrangements, especially when they recruited Welsh soldiers for the English army. This became a major source of employment and escape for the Welsh, who fought in their thousands in Scotland, France and at home too. There were nineteen thousand five hundred Welshmen serving in the royal army in 1287. Matthew Stevens has estimated this represented around a quarter of the entire Welsh male population. Such opportunities opened Welsh society up to the world as the soldiers returned with new ideas, stories and broadened horizons.

However the natives were treated, this was still a military conquest and occupation and a series of castles were built to both protect and remind people of that fact. While some now like to think that the castles are symbols of how hard it was to subdue the Welsh or how seriously the crown took the Welsh threat, it is perhaps better to see them as statements of power that spoke to both the Welsh and the English barons of the might of the Crown. They certainly went far beyond what was needed in simple military terms. They were not an iron ring that encircled the Welsh but more an iron fist that signalled how the Welsh were shattered.

With castles came new plantations of foreigners, as the policy of creating new towns of English settlers continued. Flint, Rhuddlan, Caernarfon, Conwy and Harlech all have their origins in this process, and the existing Welsh towns of Cricieth and Bere were brought into English control. These places played an important role in supplying their neighbouring castles and opening Wales up to foreign trade but they were also attempts to implant English life and English people into Wales. Moreover, they were granted monopolies on local trade meaning anyone Welsh wanting to sell their produce might be subject to un-favourable conditions. Most of Wales was too mountainous and too remote to make any form of mass settlement viable or attractive but there were isolated examples outside the towns. In Denbighshire, some ten thousand acres were given to implanted English peasants, with the pre-existing Welsh tenants being moved to infertile uplands. For some, this was probably a death sentence through starvation.

The Welsh were a conquered people and they seemed to know it. A powerful sense of national exclusion and dispossession was created that would be passed down in families. The most prosperous native Welsh town, Llanfaes in Angelsey, was demolished, as was the native abbey at Aberconwy. The few Welsh living inside the settler towns were always vulnerable and could be expelled whenever the English there decided to cut down on the competition. The Welsh found themselves looked down upon by both the English settlers and administrators brought in to govern the country. Anyone who stepped out of line was ruthlessly put down and executed if need be. It was probably the peasants who suffered the worst. Pastures and especially forests were increasingly controlled, denying people their traditional rights to hunt, gather wood and feed their animals there. Moreover, even if the conquerors did not exploit Wales as much as they might, they still saw it as somewhere to raise funds. To help finance Edward's castles and Scottish wars, new taxes were introduced which ushered in a fundamental shift in the Welsh economy as now even the peasants had to pay in cash rather than produce or labour. Such was the scale of the new taxes that by 1300 the Crown was even making a profit from Wales, despite the costs of castle building.

It was not just the fact of new taxes but also the manner of their implementation that hurt. The most powerful officials were now all English and they were not above both defrauding their lords and abusing those under their power. This could create a vicious circle because lower revenues created new pressures for additional taxes. One example of the abuses by local officials and landowners was the post-conquest evolution of a virginity tax, paid by a woman's family upon her marriage, to become a tax on known incidents of sex outside marriage. Another was how the differences between Welsh and English laws were exploited. Welsh law, for example, forbade the sale of hereditary land to protect the family inheritance. As a result, many Welsh landowners in need of money sought the right to dispose of land according to English law but were prevented from doing so unless they paid for a licence to do so. If they tried to follow the more relaxed English land laws without permission, their lords fined them for not following Welsh custom. Lords exploiting their localities through raising rents and customary fees was, of course, common in England too but the ethnic element added to the bitterness and anger it engendered. There was a real sense of dispossession and of being outsiders in their own land. Indeed, the Welsh now seemed to blame every grievance and problem on the English who acted as convenient scapegoats for all the ills of the world.

Colonisation was not a contemporary term but it does seem an apt one to describe the military occupation, the settler plantations, and the ethnic exploitation and exclusions. Unsurprisingly, simmering resentment sometimes found outlets. There were occasional revolts which saw the killing of English officials, destructions of records and

attacks on castles. Towns became a particular focus of resentment for symbolic and practical reasons. Thus, in a
revolt in 1294-5 that spread across Wales, Caernarfon
was burned, and the castellan of its castle lynched. Quite
what happened in such events is impossible to know but
it is difficult not to think of them as ethnic uprisings
against a colonial power. The 1294-95 revolt even led to
what was essentially a form of apartheid being introduced.
The Welsh were denied the right to carry arms in the
towns of north Wales, trade outside them or live inside
them. This just made things worse, feeding an undercur-
rent of ethnic tension. English residents of towns could
feel so threatened that at times they felt the Welsh wanted
them all dead. 'The Welsh are becoming arrogant and
cruel and malicious towards the English' claimed the
residents of Caernarfon in the early fourteenth century.

As in so many colonies, people did learn to live with the
new reality. Just as before the conquest, there was a
squirearchy which married across ethnic lines, adapted to
cultural differences and even learned each other's
languages. Its Welsh members increasingly tried to work
with the new political situation and to make their own
careers within it. Beyond the upper echelons of Welsh
society, there was assimilation and reconciliation too.
English governance was not immune to listening to and
acting on the complaints and grievances of its colonised
subjects. The towns were supposed to be settler societies
but, whatever the law said, in practice the Welsh were not
always excluded. In 1292-3, a third of taxpayers in
Harlech had Welsh names. A decade later, the figure for
Aberystwyth was half. In the countryside too, there was

assimilation. In time, the imported English peasantry and their ancestors began speaking Welsh. This was all part of a much wider process of assimilation. Across Europe, kingdoms were expanding, as aristocracies intermarried and increased their land holdings, and trade, religion and the movement of people eradicated some of the cultural diversity which had existed before the eleventh century. In this light, even if Wales had never been conquered, it probably would have moved closer to England in cultural and political terms. Indeed, Edward's anger at the last revolt of independent Wales owed much to how close the two nations had already become. He knew Llywelyn and his brother Dafydd well and was tied to them by marriage and family. This made their rebellion against him, and his response to it, not just political but personal too. This might explain how its harshest elements were focussed on the Gwynedd royal house.

However much reconciliation there was, it is perhaps human nature to concentrate on the wrongs rather than the rights experienced. In a society which placed so much emphasis on family history, the customs and precedents of the past, and the old prophecies of the rights of the Welsh to govern Britain, the sense of disinheritance generated by the first decades of conquest was strong and was passed down to future generations. Whereas once the Welsh felt they had lost Britain now they felt they had lost Wales too. Yet, again, this actually probably bolstered a sense of Welsh identity. The state building of the two Llywelyns may have failed but the internal Welsh rivalries that had undermined their efforts faded away with the end of the Welsh kingdoms and the common resentment of the conquest and all it brought. Most notably, actually being Welsh now had a significance for all in Wales, regardless of rank, since it could decide where they might live, where they could trade and how they might be treated by authority. Thus the racialised society conquest created brought the Welsh together by creating a common sense of an oppressed Welshness. Conquest did not kill a sense of Welsh identity but nurtured and fuelled it, showing once again how Welsh identity was defined against England.

The last national rebellion

For more than a century after conquest, the occasional violent uprisings by the Welsh never got very far, falling victim to either betrayals or the might of the English military. That was until the start of the fifteenth century and someone who became known as Owain Glyndŵr (c.1359-.c.1415). He was not a man of the people but one of the squirearchy, the minor landowning class that in status and wealth were far above the peasantry but also far below the English barons. Yet, like most of his class, his life was tied to the English and their structures of power. He had an English grandmother, his father had been an English earl's officer and he himself spent time living with an English landowning family before heading to London to learn the law. Glyndŵr even fought with the English, twice against the Scots and once against the French. Like so many of the post-conquest Welsh nobility, Glyndŵr was a man whose personal life and career advancement were intertwined with the English conquerors. That was how he and his kind had survived and even prospered.

But this did not always work and Glyndŵr failed to gain either local office or a knighthood. In the face of his stalled career, he turned to his Welsh heritage. He was a patron of the arts and Welsh poets celebrated his lineage which linked him to the royal families of three Welsh kingdoms. The Welsh bards were always rather sycophantic to those who paid them but one went as far as to claim that the Welsh faced oblivion and that Owain was the one to save them.

Whether this was what sparked his rebellion is not clear. One contemporary story claimed it began with a boundary dispute with his neighbour Lord Reginald Grey of Ruthin. Certainly, this was an age where such tensions, coupled with the kind of professional frustrations Glyndŵr had faced, could easily escalate. Reginald Grey's Ruthin was attacked, a town whose population was actually half Welsh, illustrating how from the very beginning this was not just a simple case of ethnic tensions. Nonetheless, instead of the usual burst of contained violence, something happened in 1400 that saw Glyndŵr declare himself Prince of Wales. His supporters quickly went on to attack and burn other towns in Wales, towns which were not just centres of English settlers but symbols of their privilege too, even if they did also contain Welsh inhabitants. The revolt spread, seemingly as the Welsh of all classes saw an opportunity to vent their anger at the conquest and all it meant. Across much of Wales, the squirearchy and church took up his cause. Welsh peasants and students working in England returned home to fight. Castles were attacked, although rarely held. More towns were burned. For two years, Glyndŵr waged a guerrilla war, raiding, attacking symbols and mechanisms of English power, and skirmishing with English forces.

The escalation suggested how deep-seated the resentment of conquest was, however much individuals had tried to reconcile themselves to it. But the revolt was also part of a wider period of political instability and rebellion across Europe from the mid fourteenth century. The Black Death had caused major economic upheavals, destroying the prosperity of some and emboldening others. In 1381 there had even been a major peasants' revolt in England. After seeking too much power over his barons, Richard II was dethroned in 1399 and then murdered. His successor Henry IV faced the anger, plots and rebellions of those loyal to Richard and amongst Glyndŵr's supporters were Welshmen who had prospered under the old King. Rumours of the world ending in 1400 did not help matters and the appearance of a comet in 1402 added to the general sense that something significant was happening. The English response was partly shaped by this climate and suggests that the Crown thought that this was not just another land dispute or one of the periodic outbursts of Welsh frustration. Henry IV himself led an army into Wales and stoked the fires by demanding new taxes to pay for it and exacting revenge on communities thought to support Glyndŵr. Penal Laws were passed in 1401 and 1402 that punished the Welsh and reaffirmed English dominance. They denied the Welsh the right to bear arms, to assemble for meetings, to hold public office or fortifiable houses or castles, buy land in England or property in Welsh towns. These laws even applied to Englishmen with Welsh wives. Moreover, no person of full

English blood was now to be brought to trial on the word of a Welshman. In a world where ethnicity was perceived to be something real, hierarchical and ordained by God, the Penal Laws were there to reaffirm this. The Welsh were to be put back in their place.

In practice the laws were not always applied, but they still fanned the flames of rebellion and Glyndŵr made significant progress in the spring and summer of 1402. First, he captured Reginald Grey, the Marcher lord with whom he had perhaps argued over land, and ransomed him for an immense sum which allowed the Welsh leader to transform his guerrilla rebellion into a more substantial military campaign. Then, on 22 June 1402, at Bryn Glas in Radnorshire, Glyndŵr defeated an English army, his first significant victory in an open battle. The English consoled themselves with bitter tales of how Welsh women had afterwards mutilated and castrated the English corpses. The Welsh reputation as uncivilised savages was confirmed anew, it seemed, and the Penal Laws justified.

The Battle of Bryn Glas was an important turning point in the rebellion. It emboldened Glyndŵr and saw more of the Welsh join him. The rebellion was now a war and on such a scale that English control effectively collapsed across much of Wales outside the towns. Taxes and rents often went uncollected and the legal system ground to a halt. Moreover, amongst the captured English at Bryn Glas was Edmund Mortimer, whose nephew had a strong claim to the English throne. Somehow Edmund ended up marrying Owain's daughter and joining the rebellion, giving it English allies and sucking it into an altogether different argument. If Glyndŵr's rebellion could help decide the course of English politics, then he could use that to machinate a situation from which an independent Wales might arise. A new vision emerged but one which again showed that Wales could not disentangle itself from England. He sought allies amongst England's other enemies too. His appeals for support from France led a French army to land in the south-west in 1405 and attack Haverfordwest and Carmarthen. The Scots got involved too after his appeals to their common British ancestry and shared resentment of England. But the Scots never sent more than a few soldiers and ships and, like the French support, their involvement ebbed away, leaving the Welsh to fight what had become a war for independence alone.

Owain promised to deliver the Welsh from what he called their 'oppression and captivity'. The scale of his support suggests that this was a very appealing message but not all Wales was behind him and some communities were terrorised into making payments for truces. As Owain's confidence grew, there were raids across the border to steal livestock and burn homes. The English settlements in Wales were most vulnerable and there was a hint of ethnic cleansing in the attempt to starve and drive the settlers out. Over the course of the rebellion, Glyndŵr's supporters sacked more than forty towns. Some, like Dinefwr, never recovered. The English retaliated in kind to this violence and the rebellion descended into a series of sporadic but destructive raids of burning, plundering, killing, and kidnapping. As both sides tried to stop the other feeding itself, much of the Welsh landscape and part of the borders were devastated. For all the romance associated with Glyndŵr today, there was little wistful about the starvation and ethnic violence he and his supporters inflicted and were subjected to.

Yet, alongside the destruction Glyndŵr waged, there was an emerging idea of a Welsh state with its own church, a Parliament and two universities. He negotiated with a foreign country and English barons and became as much a statesman as a rebel leader. His vision of Wales claimed lineage from the Princes of Gwynedd but it also owed much to both contemporary understandings of what a nation state looked like and to the old prophecies of a Welsh salvation. This was clear when it came to the land he claimed. His Wales followed the Severn to Worcester, taking in Hereford, and then to the 'Ash Trees of Meigion', which was between Bridgnorth in Shropshire and Kinver in Staffordshire. These trees were the place in Welsh legend where Merlin had claimed a Great Eagle would call the army of the Welsh to him.

But it was all a dream that was to prove impossible to implement or sustain once England's internal politics settled, leaving the Crown to concentrate on retaking what it had lost. In 1409, Glyndŵr lost Harlech castle, which was essentially his headquarters. He escaped, leaving his wife, two of his daughters and his grandchildren to be captured and sent to the Tower of London. The rebellion then petered out in a series of defeats and Glyndŵr disappeared from public view. Certainly, there were some in Wales who remained loyal to him but there were plenty of others tired of the poverty and suffering the war had inflicted on Welsh and English alike.

The king did not try to seek revenge. Rebels were given

pardons and an inquiry began into the conduct of royal officials in north Wales. The Crown even spent £200 buying cows and sheep for suffering tenants in Caernarfonshire and Meirionnydd. Yet reconciliation was only partial. Rebels who did not submit were hanged and some communities which had revolted were fined. The Penal Laws remained in place and although rarely implemented they symbolised how there was no ethnic equality between Welsh and English. This led some Welshmen to get Parliament to declare them English so they could reach higher office. It would be decades before the Welsh economy fully recovered from the physical and financial devastation. The psychological and cultural impact lasted much longer.

Glyndŵr was never captured and that allowed his legend to live on. The memory of him gradually shifted from the destruction his revolt had inflicted to the romance of its aspirations, feeding the old prophecies that had helped keep Wales alive in the minds of its peoples in the face of political subjugation. But that reality was now more evident than ever. Wales was reduced to an annexed land, neither assimilated nor entirely separate to England, a place where the indigenous population were looked down upon and were denied the rights of English subjects. And yet there would not be another major national rising by the Welsh. All future rebellions would be based around class rather than nation and the vast majority of the Welsh came to accept their political reality. Perhaps they still do.

Medieval Wales

Medieval history has a disproportionate importance in Wales. Its castles have become the central pillar of Welsh tourism, creating the curious situation of using products of subjugation to attract visitors and celebrate heritage. For those who yearn for an independent Wales, the medieval period provides a time to hark back to when Wales, it is alleged, was free. It provides inspiration that a national spirit can both survive conquest and colonisation and rise again in search of sovereignty. Six hundred years after Glyndŵr's rebellion, Wales was still building statues of him, naming buildings, pubs and even a university after him. This might not be a bad thing if it emboldens people to use his national spirit rather than his violence for a greater good but looking back so often to conquest and defeat also encourages a present-day idea of England as an enemy and Wales as its victim.

This is not an entirely wrong perspective, historically at least. Wales was England's first colony and it was conquered through violence. It was then subject to colonial and racialised governance. This was maybe not as oppressive as it might have been, or even as some contemporaries thought it was, but it happened nonetheless. But this is only half the story. Except for eight brief years, pre-conquest Wales was never a unified political entity. Instead, it was a collection of different kingdoms with a common cultural identity but no political unity. Moreover, they did not even think of themselves at first as Welsh but as what today we would call British. It was only when faced with the political realities and military threat of the Normans that the Welsh redefined themselves as Welsh.

And it was the Normans not the English, themselves then a conquered nation, who began the conquest of Wales. The first stage of that conquest was essentially a series of private enterprises and did not try to impose English systems of governance or merge its territories into England. That was partly because the Welsh worked with the Normans as well as against them. Even the one recognised Prince of Wales still acknowledged that he owed homage to the English crown. For all the examples of oppression, once the conflict died down, people were mostly left alone to look after their fields and livestock and to live their lives. This meant that while some learned English to get on, the vast majority of the Welsh continued to speak Welsh. Colonialism was brutal at times but it never tried to stamp out the Welsh language or Welsh identity.

Political realities explain why history mattered so much to the medieval Welsh. As it does today, history's stories, true or otherwise, sustained and even created Welsh nationhood by filling the gap left by the absence of statehood. As for nationalists today, history provided a common identity in the face of political division. Like nationalists today, the medieval Welsh also had a profound sense of historic loss, although it was first Britain and only later Wales whose loss they bemoaned. Their history was laced with prophecies that things would be different one day, that someone would come to liberate the Welsh, that they would regain their former glories. These were not just fireside tales. After the conquest, some English observers put the incessant Welsh rebellions down to these foretellings. Glyndŵr himself, may have been driven by the idea that he was the national saviour of whom the prophecies spoke.

But history has also probably left us with a misleading picture of what the medieval Welsh were actually like. Gerald of Wales, author of the first book about Wales, painted a picture of warlike people, fierce and ready to fight, committed to their freedom and defence of their country. But he was a man conditioned by his ties to the political elite of England. Was the national defiance he described the reality for peasants? Were they really more concerned with freedom than with their families and their supplies of food? Was being Welsh more important to them than being from, say, Powys or their particular corner of Powys? There is no real way of knowing. The contemporary records are dominated by the patriotic accounts of bards and vitriolic outsiders. Using these alone to understand medieval Wales is not dissimilar to relying on only the *Daily Mail* and the songs of Dafydd Iwan to understand the Wales of today.

What the contemporary sources do suggest though is that the differences between Welsh, English and Normans were seen in what today would be described as racial or ethnic terms. Although they first defined themselves as British, the Welsh were a people with a distinct identity and who were thought to have distinct characteristics. The first Norman bishop of St David's declared in the early twelfth century that the Welsh were 'entirely different in nation, language, laws and habits, judgements and customs'. The Welsh nation may have been created by historical events and a sense of difference from England but it felt very real to those inside and outside it.

Yet even then racial hierarchies could be pushed aside in day to day interactions, as peoples met, married and traded with each other. The penal codes introduced during Glyndŵr's rebellion were harsh in principle but they were often overlooked in practice and most of the towns of Wales, so often potent symbols of Welsh exclusion, were actually full of Welshmen. Even some of the Marcher lords married Welsh women to facilitate better relations and alliances with the people they ruled and neighboured. There were certainly cultural similarities rather than just differences between England and Wales. Both relied on family and the weather to survive. They lived in a Christian world and worshipped the same God. Their technologies, economies and beliefs had more in common than not. Perhaps this is the lesson that Wales today should take from its medieval past. In the face of racialised narratives, the mass of people can come together. Whatever the leaders of society are talking about, the rhythms of everyday life can produce less divisive, more peaceful realities.

II

Assimilation

Military conquest, legal apartheid and population plantations make it difficult to see medieval Wales as anything
other than a colony. But this came to an end in the middle
of the sixteenth century with the effective annexation of
Wales through two 'acts of union'. In the centuries that
followed, until the emergence of a radically different
world with industrialisation in the late eighteenth century,
there was little about Wales that seemed to be a colony.
Beyond a legal administrative structure, Wales was not
ruled differently to any part of England and the Welsh had
the same legal rights as the English. Unlike the Scots or
Irish, there was no English sense of Wales as a threat.
Politically, Wales had been assimilated into England.

This could be seen as the inevitable outcome of a
programme of colonisation, but this would be to
marginalise how the Welsh themselves saw what was
happening during that process. In their eyes, Wales was
not being obliterated but liberated and placed back at the
fore of a united Britain. Central to this was the coming to
the English throne of the Tudor family, a family which
claimed ancestral links to Welsh royalty. The perception
of the time was that the Tudors first returned to the Welsh
their prestige, then removed the legal sanctions on them,
and then gave them the word of God in their own tongue.
The sense of a British revival was then furthered in 1603

when the English and Scottish crowns were united, creating the kingdom of Great Britain. This was not accompanied by any merger of the English and Scottish legal or political systems and thus the new kingdom was, by very definition, a multinational institution. This allowed the continuation of the idea of the Welsh as a distinct nation and a people who were partners in a grander coalition.

However, the reality was that Wales was a junior partner in the new Britain. After an initial flurry of support from the Tudor monarchy, the Welsh lost their political influence on the state. With little to actually revolt against, the political threat that had existed in conquered medieval Wales had been extinguished and the nation was easily forgotten. While the oppressed Scottish Highlands were in revolt in the eighteenth century, the Welsh mountains were quiet. Nor was there anything like the turmoil that existed in Ireland. When the Scottish and Irish states were brought into formal unions with England in 1707 and 1801, their national distinction was recognised by the partial administrative and legal nature of those unions. Wales, in contrast, had been given no such recognition. The Welsh may not have felt colonised but their nation still seemed to have been politically obliterated all the same. It was not even represented on the Union Jack, the new flag developed to represent the union of the different British nations.

Yet, in both England and Wales, there continued to be a strong sense of the Welsh as a separate people. Anglicisation was a political rather than cultural process and, until industrialisation, the vast majority of ordinary

Welsh men and women could not speak English. There was no state attempt to culturally assimilate the Welsh, who were left alone, like the masses of England, to live their lives as long as they paid their taxes and did not cause political or religious trouble. They were certainly looked down upon, as ignorant, untrustworthy and uncultured, but so too was the English peasantry. In Wales, however, such attitudes encouraged the gentry to slowly turn their back on their native culture and language and, by the middle of the eighteenth century, the families and landowners that had traditionally fostered Welsh cultural and political interests were so fully assimilated into an English way of life that national differences became enmeshed with class differences.

That became particularly apparent during the processes of industrialisation that not only changed the face of Wales but moved the nation to the centre of the British economy. The injustices the new metalworks, mines and quarries inflicted on their workforces turned Wales into a crucible of political rebellion again, but the focus of resentment was now industrialists and not the state or England itself. The anger created by industrial exploitation was not easily transferred into a nationalist cause because the perpetrators were as often Welsh as English, even if they had adopted English manners and speech. Indeed, the state again showed little hostility to the idea of Wales. Certainly, the old prejudices continued but nothing much was done about them. Nonetheless, the cultural assimilation of Wales into England continued apace in the industrial era as the Welsh people saw the English language as a way to escape the industrial and rural poverty all around them.

The creation of a union

For another century or so after Glyndŵr's rebellion, Wales remained a colony of England. However, in the east and south, it was still the Marcher lords rather than the king who ruled. Their political transgressions, along with some untimely deaths and failures to produce sons, meant their number was dwindling and their lands gradually passing to the Crown. But this did not change the March's reputation for unlawfulness and as a sanctuary for criminals. It was an exaggerated reputation but its lords did milk their landholdings financially and neglect their duties to oversee and maintain daily governance. This actually empowered the Welsh gentry who held junior positions of local responsibility across Wales and the March, despite the penal codes introduced during Glyndŵr's rebellion. Such jobs tied the gentry to England and many intermarried with families across the border and adopted English surnames. Their land holdings grew and the Welsh economic and social structure became more like that of England.

But the Welsh gentry remained Welsh in speech and thought and this made them vulnerable. Those who became unpopular or got in the way of anyone English in the district could be cast aside on the basis of their ethnicity, which was set in law as a second-class identity. Some applied to the state to be recognised as English to avoid this fate. In contrast, English landowners implanted after the conquest were gradually taking the opposite route, as they gradually internalised a Welsh identity and intermarried with neighbouring Welsh families. This in itself was a suggestion that the anti-Welsh laws were not routinely implemented and that Wales' colonial status was far from straightforward.

Nonetheless, there was a growing sense in the fifteenth century that the Welsh were being denied opportunities for social advancement and that the country's administration was a mess. Legal arrangements across Wales and the March were certainly complex. In some districts, English law was used but in other places Welsh law was followed. At times, it depended on which would suit the interests of those in power locally. Welsh law had evolved after conquest, taking on forms from its English equivalent. Gradually, Welsh law made more use of juries and capital punishment and less use of compensatory justice (where victims were compensated rather than perpetrators punished). But some in Wales wanted further reforms. The concept of inheritance being divided between sons was particularly unpopular because it hampered Welsh gentry families in their attempts to build up stronger and larger estates.

Welsh complaints about their treatment and the operation of law were taken more seriously after the victory of Henry Tudor (1457-1509) at the Battle of Bosworth. This saw the accession to the English throne of a man who claimed a Welsh ancestry. In reality, this was rather limited; his grandfather was from Anglesey and claimed a Welsh noble descent stretching back into medieval times, but the other three sides of Henry's family were English or French. Nonetheless, Henry was born in Pembroke and raised there and in Raglan. In pursuing financial and practical support for his rather tenuous claim to the English throne, Henry exploited his Welsh connections and the poetic prophecies that a saviour would restore Britain to the Welsh and free them from their subjugation. He even fought at Bosworth under a flag bearing the red dragon and his victory was an immense psychological boost for the Welsh. Henry declared himself, 'by the grace of god, King of England and of France, Prince of Wales and Lord of Ireland'. This was a break from the custom that reserved the Welsh title for their heir to the English throne and it perhaps hints that his sense of attachment ran deeper than pragmatic politics. Whatever it meant, Henry's Welsh supporters were rewarded and his ascension to the throne meant there was a feeling that the prophecies had been realised and there was a step change in the relationship between Wales and England. The Welsh writer George Owen of Henllys (c.1552-1613) called Henry 'the Moses who delivered us from bondage'. The king continued to make symbolic nods to Wales, naming his son Arthur and adding a red dragon to his royal arms.

Under Henry VII, it became easier for Welshmen to rise up political and social ladders but they remained, in theory at least, disadvantaged in law. In various places, the penal codes introduced after Glyndŵr were formally abolished, but since communities sometimes had to pay for this, it was hardly an act of magnanimity by a king to his compatriots. Indeed, by the reign of Henry's son, Henry VIII, for the commoners the consequences of simply being Welsh were actually getting worse, at least if they broke, or were suspected of breaking, the law, something which in itself was a complicated question because of how Welsh and English law co-existed. In an attempt to improve law and order, Rowland Lee, the bishop of Lichfield, was made president of the Council of Wales in 1534. This, in effect, gave him control of the March and he set about trying to bring it to order with relish. He attributed the lawlessness and theft common in the March to the natural inclinations of the Welsh and his solution was brutal. He simply hanged those who broke the law and one contemporary claimed, with probably a degree of exaggeration, that five thousand men suffered this fate under Lee in six years.

In 1534, Henry VIII, having failed to get his marriage annulled, made himself rather than the Pope head of the church in England. In the resulting political tension, Wales was seen to make England vulnerable. It contained disgruntled, ambitious men unhappy at their ethnic disadvantage and the legal complexities of their homeland. Moreover, Wales was also geographically close to Catholic Ireland and a potential landing place for any invading foreign force, just as it had been for Henry VII.

It was Thomas Cromwell, the crown's chief minister, who acted to solve the problem. He was engaged in a programme of reform to strengthen and unify the English state, ridding it of historical anomalies, administrative untidiness and potential fissures that might cause political unrest and legal uncertainty. Wales was certainly one such anomaly and fissure, as the Crown was only too aware given the complaints of Welshmen. Cromwell's solution was what historians centuries later would call the Acts of Union and what some today regard as an attempt to annexe, assimilate or even abolish Wales altogether.

There were actually two Acts of Union. The first came in 1536 but was unclear and ill-defined and thus it was supplemented by a second act in 1542-43. The modern-day criticisms are borne out by the preamble to the first act which declared that Wales was 'for ever from henceforth incorporated, united and annexed to and with this ... realm of England'. The contradictions of the Act were evident in the fact that it also stated this state of incorporation, annexation and unity was already the case and 'ever hath been'. In the Principality political and administrative assimilation was already far gone and for this reason alone the Acts have an unfair reputation. In some ways, the Acts were not primarily about uniting Wales and England at all but rather the Principality and the March in order to end the different administrative structures and patchwork of different legal jurisdictions within Wales. The Acts achieved this by abolishing Welsh law. It was already in retreat and this change was far from as radical as sometimes still made out. More importantly, the March was abolished and the Principality expanded to cover the whole of Wales (minus Monmouthshire). This not only had the benefit for the State of creating a simpler administrative structure, it also made Wales easier to levy taxes from.

Some of the Acts' clauses have become embedded in how we think about Wales today. The counties of Anglesey, Caernarfonshire, Cardiganshire, Carmarthenshire, Flintshire and Merionethshire had been created after the conquest but now they were added to as the March was divided up into Breconshire, Denbighshire, Glamorgan, Montgomeryshire, Pembrokeshire and Radnorshire. The creation of these counties also established the border between Wales and England. This was done on the basis of landholdings and parishes with the result that some parts of Wales were transferred to Shropshire and Herefordshire. This included Welsh-speaking communities such as Oswestry, a place that had always been considered Welsh, but, since the act ensured that Wales and England were to be treated the same, this made little difference in the short term, even if it was to have profound impact on their identity in the longer term.

Had the Acts been imposed on an unwilling Welsh people then they could be considered colonial acts but they were not. The poor probably knew nothing of them but the Welsh gentry welcomed the legislation. Indeed, the preamble to the second act said that the King 'of his tender zeal and affection that he beareth towards his loving and obedient subjects' in Wales was enacting the law in response to their 'humble suit and petition'. This did rather overlook what the king and his state got out of the acts but it was true in that he was responding to demand. Nor are the acts comparable with the act of union with Scotland which was passed by the parliaments of both nations. As a colony, Wales had no Parliament to give its consent. Nonetheless, one thing the first act did do was give Wales representation in Parliament and thus the second act was passed by a body containing Welsh members. Those representatives were fully behind the legislation. For them and the wider gentry, the key issue was not the political union of England and Wales, something which in essence already existed, but the removal of the legal disadvantages of being Welsh. They saw the legislation not as acts of assimilation but of liberation that ended the system of apartheid and the system of Welsh law which they felt was old-fashioned and disadvantageous.

Now, everyone in Wales had the same legal status regardless of ethnicity. As the first act put it, 'Persons, born and to be born in the said Principality, Country or Dominion of Wales, shall have, enjoy and inherit all and singular Freedoms, Liberties, Rights, Privileges and Laws within this Realm, and other King's Dominions, as other the King's Subjects naturally born within the same have, enjoy and inherit.'

Nonetheless, the acts inevitably had consequences for the idea of a Wales as nation. They cemented the political assimilation of Wales but they also paved the way for the long-term emergence of a civic rather than ethnic vision of the nation. Now the ancestry of anyone living in Wales did not matter in any legal sense, the path was cleared for everyone living in Wales to be considered Welsh. Moreover, the legislation still acknowledged that Wales was different; despite establishing political unity, the 1536 Act still referred to Wales as a 'dominion, principality and country'. Thus the acts contained an inherent contradiction of both acknowledging Welsh difference and bringing to an end the political and legal consequences of that difference. Wales was still even to be subject to a different system of administrative governance. The second act created a Great Session of Wales, a circuit of judges for Wales, but this excluded Monmouthshire, seemingly just to ensure the neatness of twelve counties divided into four equal sized circuits of courts. This too would have long-term significance for the identity of that county.

The view of Wales as 'different' was also clear in a passage that declared Welsh was 'nothing like nor consonant to the natural mother tongue'. As part of the legislation's goal of administrative unity across the kingdom, English was made the language of courts, although in practice this was probably already the norm. It also required that those holding public office be able to speak English, again something that was probably already standard practice. Neither clause meant the Acts were deliberately trying to abolish Welsh. Indeed, in practice, banishing Welsh entirely from either the courts or public administration would have been impossible since the majority of people subject to it were monoglot Welsh. But the symbolic and practical disadvantages to those who only spoke Welsh were probably significant and it must have created some sense amongst the Welsh monoglot majority that they were being denied equal justice with English speakers. The mass of people, or at least those who encountered the law, thus perhaps came to see what the gentry already knew. To get on in a society where power lay in England, speaking English was a significant advantage. Yet, once the previously-enshrined disadvantages of being Welsh fell away after the Acts of Union, the language actually regained ground in Welsh towns and rural anglicised areas such as the lowlands of Gwent and Glamorgan. The status of English may have been reinforced by the Acts of Union but Welsh remained the language of the land and the people.

The Welsh language, along with the wild landscape and underdeveloped rural economy ensured that the Welsh remained, in early modern English eyes, an uncivilised, strange people. Given the religious turmoil of the era, this continued to cause concern even after the first Act of Union. In 1541 Christ's College, Brecon was created to try and educate some of the Welsh in the ways of the English so as to strengthen their religious adherence to the new protestant Church of England. Yet more significant was how religious concerns drew the state towards supporting rather than oppressing the Welsh language. In 1546, John Prys of Brecon had published the first book in the Welsh language. In it were the Credo, the Lord's Prayer and the Ten commandments. The Pope did not approve of such attempts to open the scriptures up to the people but they did appeal to the Crown's ongoing battles with Rome. It sanctioned the creation of an English prayer book in 1549 and two years later parts of it were translated into Welsh. In 1567, a Welsh translation of the New Testament was published. It had been led by the Bishop of St David's but the impetus came from the Crown who ordered that a Welsh bible be put in every parish church in order to ensure that all parts of the kingdom were worshipping in the same way. Spiritual needs thus trumped linguistic ones and the same state that twenty or so years before had made English the language of administration in Wales now ensured that Welsh was a language of religion.

Or at least this was the short-term intention. English-language bibles were also required to be available in Welsh churches in the hope that they would be used too. But there was little need for that. The word of God could now be listened to in Welsh and births, marriages and deaths blessed in the people's own tongue. This gave the language a status and relevance in the life of the masses that far exceeded anything that happened in the remote world of governance. Yet some modern writers have seen the translation of the Bible into Welsh as a colonial act, intended to extend English influence in Wales. It did ensure that Wales followed England's new Protestantism rather than Catholicism. Thus, in what was the biggest social division of the day, Wales was on the side of England rather than the French, Spanish or Irish. Ultimately, this common Protestantism and the fear of Catholic invasion, which for the Welsh was very plausible given how close Ireland was, helped bind the British nations together in the longer term. Yet whatever the political consequences, the state's action in allowing the translation of the Bible and prayer book buttressed Welsh, giving the language a status, both culturally and in the written word, perhaps preventing its falling away into an oral vernacular. This helps explain why the language fared better than Irish and Gaelic, which did not see their own versions of the Bible until 1690 and 1801.

While the state was unintentionally helping save the Welsh language, the Welsh were setting about making the most of opportunities in England now any legal ethnic barrier to them had been removed. Careers in law and politics lured more and more well-off Welshmen to England, especially since Wales had no university of its own. The result was that in the later sixteenth and seventeenth centuries there was a sprinkling of Welsh men or men from Welsh families across the highest offices of England. No longer sometimes excluded by the nationality, the comfortably off in Wales chose to ally themselves with rather than against the union. Thus, a desire for personal social progress welded the Welsh gentry to England and the English state. Geography and family ties continued to do the same. The mountainous distance between north and south meant Welsh families looked east for marriages rather than within Wales, something easier now the taint of being Welsh had been mostly removed. If there had been any lingering hope of restoring Welsh independence after Glyndŵr, the Acts of Union had killed it by enlarging the English ties of Wales' native internal leadership.

Yet their anglicisation was a very slow process that both predated the Acts of Union and was far from complete more than a century afterwards. It would thus be wrong to blame the Acts alone for the Welsh gentry's anglicisation. The reality was that speaking English and seeking careers in England were already important to them. If anything, the Acts freed the Welsh gentry to celebrate their Welshness. They continued to patronise Welsh poetry and music until the end of the seventeenth century. They fostered and encouraged a new interest in the history of Welsh as the original Britons. This was used to not only justify the current political arrangements but the expansion of English power too. Out of the interest in Wales' past came the story of a Prince Madoc who had allegedly discovered America in around 1170. It was almost certainly a myth but it was widely circulated because it helped legitimise the idea that Elizabeth I had the right to colonise America. Welsh history may have been used to bolster the union and English expansionism, but this still gave Wales a central place in English politics and thus it also fed a Welsh identity, engendering a pride that the Welsh people had been restored to their place at the head of the island. Since it was the monarchy that had delivered this, it was little wonder that the Welsh gentry were overwhelmingly Royalist in the misnamed 'English' civil war of 1642 to 1651.

In 1603, James VI of Scotland was crowned James I of England. The old prophecies now seemed complete; Britain was one again and under the rule of its native peoples. This also opened the way for the emergence of a new understanding of Britishness as a multinational entity, but it would be one in which Wales was very clearly the junior partner. Indeed, now that Britain was under one ruler, Wales was less useful to the state since the legitimacy it offered for a wider British union was no longer needed. Through the seventeenth century, the anglicisation of Welsh gentry thus gathered pace. More and more adopted English as their main language and came to value power and landownership more than the historic Welsh obsession with ancestry and pedigree. They continued to think of themselves as Welsh but that was not where their political allegiance lay. Their desire for social progress and a shared fear of Catholicism ensured that. Wales was thus reduced to a curious appendage of England with its own identity, while the Welsh language was becoming the tongue of the common people rather than those of status. This was to have significant long-term consequences. It added a linguistic dimension to class divisions and weakened the written form of Welsh and the language's use in arenas which might have given it a status that would prevent future generations questioning its value.

As Welsh increasingly became just the language of the common people, new prejudices towards it developed in England. In 1682, a book entitled *Wallography or the Briton Described* was published. It was a satirical account of a journey through Wales. Despite its intended humour, it revealed how the Welsh, with their 'native gibberish' were still seen as profoundly different to the English. They were a people to be laughed and sneered at but, in an unstable world still afraid of Popish threats and the unknown, the Welsh were unsettling too. This was also evident in Daniel Defoe's 1720s account of travelling through the country. He described both the Welsh mountains and their names as 'barbarous' and expressed his surprise at finding somewhere in Britain where the inaccessibility and 'terror' of the Alps was exceeded. But he also noted how he found the Welsh gentry civil and generous. This was partly because they looked after him and spoke to him but it should not be imagined that this meant they were entirely anglicised. Defoe also noted how much they valued 'their antiquity' and their ancient heroes such as 'Prince Lewellin'.

As the size of the educated class expanded, the tradition of looking to the past to foster Welsh patriotism was revived and, from the late seventeenth century, there was a new interest in the nation's antiquity. This gathered pace in the following century or so because it helped compensate for the decline of distinctive Welsh poetry, music and customs in an age of industrialisation, religious puritanism and the Anglicisation of the upper classes. The history of the language, the landscape and the people all found new scholars and the term 'Celtic' was used for the first time to describe the culture and language of the Welsh, Scots, Irish, Cornish and Bretons. Not all the scholarship was rooted in the actual past. Most notable was Theophilus Evans, a curate in Breconshire. In 1716 he wrote a book called *Drych y Prif Oesoedd* (*The Mirror of Past Ages*), which claimed the Welsh were descended from Noah. He was outdone however by Edward Williams, better known as Iolo Morganwg, who forged medieval Welsh poetry and invented the Gorsedd of the Bards, a society of poets and others who dressed in robes and conducted their own rituals, in an attempt to link modern Wales to the druids of Roman times. In the nineteenth century, his invention would become a mainstay of the National Eisteddfod. Such ideas, and the very concept of the Welsh as Celts, mattered, because they reaffirmed Wales as different to England. But more than that it also affirmed their roots in the islands as predating the English, making them the true Britons with a romantic and mysterious image to boot. The historical reality of the term and the ideas that went with it were not the point. It was their effect and power in the present that mattered. History was once again giving the Welsh a sense of self-esteem and a unique identity.

Such stories were attractive in England too, where an era of romanticism was emerging in the late eighteenth century. War meant the continent was no longer as safe as it once had been and the curious turned their eyes closer to the home. Like far-off places in the growing British Empire, the 'Celts' at home were safe exotics to be wondered at and even visited. The wild landscapes of Wales, with its barbaric names and frightening mountains, were no longer seen as threatening and unsettling, as they had been for Defoe, but rather beautiful, timeless and picturesque. As the first stages of industrialisation emerged and the present offered the unsettling political realities of revolution in America and French, the medieval past was rediscovered as a place of chivalry where status and rank mattered. For the first time, Wales' history and castles were attractive to outsiders.

Just as in the medieval period, whether any of these questions of nationality mattered much to the mass of the Welsh people is a different matter. They endured continual toil and subsistence living, surely worrying more about their crops, health and souls than their nationality. But that does not mean being Welsh was irrelevant. Any encounter with authority would have been a reminder that they spoke a different language from the instruments of state, adding an ethnic dimension to the tensions of class. How they felt about this is shrouded in uncertainty, since their status denied them a written voice, but it is difficult not to conclude that it must have mattered in some way.

Industry and Empire

In the century or so after the Acts of Union, the key instrument of assimilation was not law but simple economics. Better law and order helped trade. Farming developed and slowly the landscape was further cleared of trees and enclosed into fields. Cattle and wool were Wales' key products but, since the country lacked any large town, the primary markets were England's western towns. Thus, even in the early modern period, there was no Welsh economy as such and instead its surpluses were sold to England. It was here that today's complaint about Wales' transport network being orientated towards England has its origins. The first major roads did indeed run to England rather than within Wales, but this was not because the state was extracting what it needed but because the Welsh were looking for places to sell what they had. Moreover, to judge the Welsh transport network through roads (or railways) is to miss one of its central components. The sea was on three sides of Wales whereas England was only on one. Through the oceans Wales had access to the world, meaning there was little need to look at how to develop internal communications. The Welsh never developed a Welsh economy because they did not need one.

The sea was key to the development of the coal industry in the seventeenth century. There was little demand for coal in Wales since the mineral's major consumers, manufacturers of bricks, soap and glass, were few in number. It was thus primarily dug in places close to the coast – notably Swansea, south Pembrokeshire and Flintshire – and then shipped to Ireland, south-west England and France. Such trade saw Welsh towns slowly grow, even if they remained small compared to England. That growth was based on a population migrating from the countryside. Wales' towns thus gradually became more Welsh speaking as the Welsh themselves now colonised what had once been colonial plantations.

The early digging of coal was a forerunner of how external economic needs transformed Wales in the eighteenth century and made it one of the first industrial nations in the world. Key to that was Wales' ready supplies of metal ores and the coal needed to smelt them. The first major industries to develop were copper and lead smelting in Swansea and Neath. Then, in northern Glamorgan and Monmouthshire, came iron, a product used to build everything from cannons to railways. Then, in the nineteenth century, the coal industry mushroomed across the south and north-east, as the age of steam emerged. Much of the coal from the Glamorgan valleys was very high in quality, burning easily but without giving off much smoke. This made it particularly desirable for navies who did not want their ships given away by trails of smoke. But it was also important for railways, and Welsh coal was sought after across the globe. By 1898, coal from south Wales accounted for almost a fifth of the entire British coal industry's output and labour force.

Industrialisation happened at a frightening pace and its impact was felt far and wide. There was work aplenty for men and women and the country's population exploded from six hundred thousand in 1801 to nearly two and a half million in 1911. Villages and scattered farming communities became large bustling towns in a few decades. The Rhondda saw its population grow from under a thousand in 1851 to more than a hundred and fifty thousand by 1911. There and elsewhere, rivers turned black; landscapes changed from a lush greenness to scarred, smoky and polluted vistas. The ports grew too, as coal was sent around the globe and grain was imported in vast quantities. In a century, Cardiff changed from being a small market town to one of the most important industrial shipping ports in the world. Most of Wales remained rural but it was not untouched. Growing towns created new demands for foods and wools thus sharing out some of the industrial wealth to rural villages. Industrial communities were magnets for the young seeking to replace rural poverty with excitement and better pay. Across

Wales, towns were vibrant societies with a plethora of educational, intellectual, sporting, musical and, of course, drinking venues. Whereas once those seeking better lives had headed for England, now there was plenty to keep them in Wales and that helped protect the Welsh language. But most of the industrial opportunities were concentrated in the south and north-east. Industrialisation thus made Wales very lopsided, changing it from the pre-eighteenth century situation where the population was distributed across its counties fairly evenly to one where Glamorgan and Monmouthshire held sway. This created an inequity and imbalance with which Wales still struggles. Some rural parts continue to be marginalised by their lack of population, whereas the former coalfields have a large population but no longer the economy that first put it there.

The historian John Williams has suggested that Wales was not fully industrialised because it lacked a manufacturing base and was instead centred on producing materials that would be used elsewhere. Perhaps only in the production of woollen garments was Wales making things on a large scale from local resources. The economy in Wales was also very male with, for example, 807,600 men in formal employment in 1911 but only 215,700 women. This masked much wider levels of female economic contributions but almost half of female jobs were in service, illustrating the narrow parameters of Welsh industry.

Domestic service was at least serving Welsh needs whereas wider Welsh industrialisation was driven by external needs. This meant it did not create a Welsh economy. Instead, it strengthened the existing economic ties between Wales and England, and encouraged better transport communications between the two countries, although it also saw canals and railways built to link the centre of Wales to its ports. England came psychologically closer too with the construction of telegraph networks which enabled commercial and political news to be sent by electrical pulse in seconds. The industrial revolution even merged Wales into London's time zone. Traditionally, everywhere had used local time based on the sun which could vary by up to half an hour from London. Railways complicated this because places far apart were brought within easy travelling distance. At first, the solution was to advertise departure times but not those for arrival. But, in 1847, the British rail companies came together and agreed to run trains by Greenwich Mean Time rather than local time. This was then enforced by law in 1880 and another aspect of regional diversity in the UK was lost to commercial needs.

It is often said that industrialisation created an extractive economy in Wales. It was certainly centred on something literally taken from the ground but there are also widespread claims today that the wealth this generated was extracted from Wales too. Industrialisation was a private revolution rather than a state one and thus if the wealth generated by industry did leave the country it was not the doing of the government. The investment and drive for the first wave of industrialisation, especially in the iron industry, did come from English entrepreneurs who saw the possibilities which the easy availability of iron ore and charcoal in the region offered to meet the demand of the British war machine's need for metals.

Since the capital came from England, it would be easy to think that was where all the profits went too. But the English industrialists who developed the Welsh iron industry often settled around the source of their wealth. The Crawshay family, for example, came from Yorkshire but, after making a fortune from their ironworks around Merthyr, built Cyfarthfa Castle and it became the family seat. However they viewed their own nationality, they became part of Welsh society and, despite living off the labour of their workforce, they did sponsor philanthropic ventures in the communities they had helped create. Charlotte Guest, the wife of another Merthyr iron magnate, even learned Welsh and translated the *Mabinogion* into English.

Moreover, industrialisation was not an entirely English affair. In the early stages of the industrial revolution, for example, the development of copper mines on Anglesey owed much to Thomas Williams, a lawyer from the island. The development of the coal industry too owed much to Welshmen. Indeed, most of the largest coal companies in Wales were set up by Welsh entrepreneurs. David Davies (1818-90), for example, started life working in his father's sawpit in Llandinam but his business ventures saw him become the hugely wealthy owner of the Ocean Coal Company. Like others, he built himself a mansion in Wales. His family wealth thus remained in Wales and one by-product of it is the collection of impressionist art collected by his daughters and now on display at the National Museum of Wales.

Whether any Welsh industrial owner paid or treated his workers any better than his English peers is doubtful. The slate magnate Lord Penrhyn claimed ancestry going back to the lords of medieval Wales but his quarries were still home to a bitter dispute over unionisation and work practices that lasted from 1900 to 1903 and which split the community when some were tempted back to work and rewarded with pay rises. Capitalism was capitalism, regardless of the nation perpetuating it. Thus those who argue that Wales' natural resources were taken from it are only telling a partial truth. The people of Wales never owned the bulk of the resources of the land. It was not another nation that denied them but an economic system of capitalism. Moreover, nor was all the wealth generated by industry concentrated in the hands of the capitalists. Industry did not just fund the stately homes of its owners or the reconstruction of Cardiff Castle or Castell Coch but also the miners' welfare halls, the sporting grounds and theatres, and even the very existence of jobs. Mining may have been harsh and dangerous work but in the 1890s average wages in the south Wales coal industry were double that of Glamorgan agricultural workers.

That industrialisation should not be seen as a case of national exploitation is evident from the fact that people at the time did not make this argument. The workers of Wales did not take their situation sitting down, but they saw the social cleavage that they were at the wrong end of as one of class rather than nationhood. In 1831, the workers of Merthyr rebelled against wage cuts and at the way their debts were being administered and recovered. Against a background over wider tensions as to who should have the vote, they armed themselves, took control of the town, spoke of the French revolution and raised the red flag. The army was sent in and at least sixteen were killed in the resulting violence. The 1820s and 1830s were also the years of the Scotch Cattle, a secret movement of sorts that used a combination of disguise, ritual and violence to terrify into compliance those who broke local conceptions of sexual, economic and community morality. The Rebecca Riots of 1839-43 in Pembrokeshire and Carmarthenshire also employed disguises in their attacks on the tollgates used to charge them for travelling the roads to and from their farms. The spark may have been economic but the protestors diversified the object of their attentions to workhouses and to fathers not supporting their children. More straightforwardly political were the Chartists who demanded the vote and a new democracy. A petition to Parliament in 1839 got nowhere and what seems to have been an attempt at starting a revolution saw an armed march on Newport. When the first Chartists arrived in the town, the army opened fire and twenty-two died.

These were all revolts of the working class rather than of the Welsh but it should not be imagined that nationality played no role. The fact that the people spoke a different language and had a different religion to their masters surely fuelled the fires of resentment. Language, after all, defines how people process and articulate their feelings. It is central to how people conceive of themselves and their place in the world. Any alienation this might have created would have been strongest when dealing with the law. Even if they came up before a Welsh-speaking judge, English was the language of the courts and that surely made some feel they were being denied justice or disadvantaged by their language. Such situations were not just limited to criminals or political agitators. In the middle of the nineteenth century, there were Welsh-speaking families thrown off their land for not voting the way their English-speaking landlords told them to, or because they stood in the way of attempts to enclose land or exploit its minerals. In the 1820s, one such case in Cardiganshire turned violent and became known as Rhyfel y Sais Bach (the war of the little Englishman) in reference to the English landowner whose home had been destroyed by angry locals. Such incidents may have created a sense that nationality and language were part of the problem people faced but similar disturbances happened in England too, which was also experiencing a period of strikes and revolt, and whose own courts also rarely favoured the ordinary man or woman. Across Britain, out of a longstanding popular belief in fairness, came a sense of class consciousness as industrial and agricultural workers alike felt they were being exploited. But oppression in England does not change the fact that the Welsh masses were often disadvantaged by being both Welsh and working class. Today this would get called intersectionality, a grand term to describe the very real coalescence of social and cultural hierarchies.

That the mass of the Welsh people were not simply willing to be exploited is further evidenced by how willing they were to move to better their lives. This played a decisive role in pushing forward the cultural assimilation of Wales that had made little ground before industrialisation. Until the 1870s the majority of migrants to coal and iron communities came from Wales. But people were also being attracted from the west of England and, from the 1870s to the First World War, the English were the biggest migrant group into the coalfield. Indeed, between 1871 and 1911, two hundred and twenty thousand people moved from England into Glamorgan. By that latter year, more than half of people in the county were born outside Wales or had at least one parent who had been.

Immigration from England into industrial Wales was not without tension. In Mold in 1869, anger over inequalities in wages between Welsh and imported English miners escalated into violence. A crowd stoned a military escort taking two Welsh miners to prison for assaulting an English manager. The soldiers returned fire, killing two colliers and two women. A coroner's jury declared the deaths 'justifiable homicide' and the local press and authorities supported the military's action. Wider reactions demonstrated some of the hostility towards the Welsh that had helped spark the tensions in the first place. The area was portrayed in the English press as an unlawful place and the *Saturday Review* even claimed the Welsh language resembled 'the growl of animals' more than 'the articulate speech of civilised men'. As a result, it thought the Welsh were debarred from 'an exchange of thought with their neighbours and fellow subjects' and thus continued to 'vent their traditionary hates, antipathies and prepossessions in sounds which the rest of the world can neither understand nor imitate'. It concluded there was a hereditary national dislike of the English. This was all an extreme example but it may be that there were a host of daily tensions that are lost to the historical record. In the 1880s one teacher in Glamorgan reported that teaching

Welsh would lessen the 'petty jealousy between the races' in the area. Yet the shared experience of work and community were powerful unifying factors that seem to have been more important than any cultural or linguistic tension. The Welsh and English lived, worked and played alongside each other with seemingly few problems. It was little surprise that they intermarried too and when they did it was often English that the family decided to raise the children in.

An easy supply of labour from the east illustrated how being part of Britain was key to how and why Welsh industry developed so fast and so far. England's growing power overseas had also opened doors to global trades and capital ventures, including the money to be made from slavery. The Welsh have to accept their share of blame for this atrocity and there were even slave plantations in the Caribbean with names like Swansea and Denbigh. After Britain took control of Trinidad from Spain in 1797, it was a Welshman from Haverfordwest, Thomas Picton, who was appointed the island's governor. Under his rule, any of the island's ten thousand slaves who rebelled were dealt with viciously, and he was even successfully tried for having used torture to extract a confession from a thirteen-year-old charged with robbery. Other Welsh families had significant investments in plantations and made huge profits from them, even if they never saw a slave first hand. The development of the copper, iron and slate industries in Wales all owed something to profits made in Caribbean plantations. Notably, the Penrhyn slate quarries were developed with family money made through slavery. Welsh industrial jobs were thus created on the back of slave labour. Even rural workers benefited indirectly from this evil since a major market for their cheap wool was slave plantations. British imperialism enabled the growth of Welsh industries in other ways too. It was the military and political tensions that sprung from British overseas expansion that provided much of the initial impetus for the Welsh metal industries since iron was needed for cannons and copper for the bottom of ships. The coal industry centred on exports and it was British imperial power that ensured access to global markets. Vast numbers of Welsh jobs were thus made and sustained by Empire.

It could be argued that everyone in Britain, no matter how humble or what their nationality, benefited directly from Empire, even if only because it gave them access to cheap and sometimes exotic foods to eat and drink. But Empire was also a cultural concept; it affected how people thought and gave the British a sense of superiority, power and even sometimes destiny. Historians argue over how true this was for the working classes but, like a sense of Welshness, it was there in the backdrop of life and people's minds. Moreover, for the Welsh, for so long an oppressed people, the idea that they were at the centre of the world's most powerful and civilised empire was perhaps seductive. More prosaically, the Empire provided employment and excitement overseas. Those involved from Wales were not just the well off and they could be found in every corner of the Empire. The Welsh were ad-ministrators, soldiers, explorers, fortune seekers, missionaries, or simply settlers. In the nineteenth century, more than one hundred and twenty thousand Welsh men and women emigrated in search of better lives for themselves, although the most popular destination, the USA, was no longer part of the Empire. Sometimes the Welsh were specifically invited to come to places that needed their industrial and technical skills. They may not have thought of themselves as colonialists, but their movement contributed to the direct and indirect oppression of the cultures and very lives of the indigenous peoples of Australia, New Zealand, Canada and elsewhere. These migrants wrote home and their letters were often printed in Welsh newspapers. This kept the Empire in sight and ensured it was not just an abstract concept but somewhere where neighbours and family could be found.

Perhaps the most self-consciously Welsh group in the Empire were the missionaries. Welsh Nonconformists travelled the Empire, preaching their version of Christianity to those under British rule. Some felt that being Welsh actually made them more sympathetic imperialists because they understood what it meant to be colonised. It is easy to be romantic about these missionaries and their educational and charitable work but their attempts to spread Christianity were indeed part of a colonial project. They helped undermine local cultures and contributed to the climate in colonised places that saw Western culture as more civilised and encouraged locals to follow their conquerors.

The Welsh even had their own colony. In 1865, one hundred and sixty-five Welsh men, women and children settled in Patagonia after having negotiated rights to some land with the Argentine government who were looking for European settlers to develop and civilise their fledgling nation. In time, the first settlers were joined by others from Wales and a Welsh community was established. Like so many emigrants, they went in search of better lives but, unlike others, they also had a nationalist objective. They sought the dignity, autonomy and sovereignty they felt they did not have at home and in doing so revealed how at least some Welsh people in the middle of the nineteenth century still regarded themselves as oppressed. Yet they also had an awareness that the blame for the situation in Wales could not just be accorded to England but owed something to sentiment within Wales too. Michael D. Jones, the inspiration behind the project, wrote of 'an enslaved nation… which deteriorates to such a point that it wants to destroy its own inheritance, national language and customs.' Escaping this and creating a new Welsh society was not possible in other colonies because, as they knew from personal experience of trying life in the USA, the English language inevitably dominated there. Thus, to make a free Welsh-speaking society, they needed to make their own colony.

Today, many like to celebrate Patagonia, if only because it represents the only Welsh-speaking community outside Wales, but it was colonialism nonetheless, even if that was what the Welsh settlers thought they themselves were trying to escape from. Their allotted lands were in areas populated and controlled by different indigenous peoples who had been compensated by the government in return for acknowledging Argentine sovereignty and behaving peacefully to the settlers. This they did, helping the Welsh survive a harsh climate, poor soil and pumas. But the natives' friendship and co-operation did not change the fact that control of their traditional lands had been lost. Moreover, like so many colonialists everywhere, the Welsh initially held onto their identities rather than assimilated into their host society. Even the Welsh name chosen for the new settlement summed up what it was, Y Wladfa, the colony.

The Welsh colonists were aware of this irony, even before arriving, but they went ahead anyway. Their solution was to be fair and just towards the indigenous peoples and they did try to follow this maxim in trade and other relations. Yet their letters home showed that they thought themselves superior and more civilised than the people on whose lands they lived. As Lucy Taylor has argued, the Welsh in Patagonia benefited from the global hierarchies of race and civilisation. This was clear in their dealings with the Argentine government who also deemed the Welsh to be set above the indigenous population. The government extended its direct governance over Patagonia and tried to build its own sense of nationhood through enforcing Spanish education, but it did not stop the Welsh using their language and keeping their traditions. In contrast, the government's treatment of the indigenous people was becoming increasingly brutal. In 1882, the Argentinian army arrived in the Welsh colony and killed and interned indigenous peoples as part of a national project for the expansion of Argentine governance. The Welsh were horrified and protested but even in this they were not unusual in terms of European colonisers who sometimes had a paternal sense of protection towards the people they conquered, as long as those people were pliant and unthreatening.

It was not just encounters overseas that showed how integration into the British Empire had created a sense of racial superiority amongst the Welsh. Imperialism also brought people from across the world to Wales. Cardiff, Swansea and Newport were all major international ports and that meant a constant stream of sailors from all around the world. Some chose to settle and those Welsh ports were among the most diverse places in the UK. By 1911, Cardiff had the second highest proportion of foreign-born male residents anywhere in Britain, Swansea the fourth, and Newport the sixth. This category did not include those born in the Empire, a group that amounted to some thirteen hundred people in Cardiff. Some made their way inland in search of work and a small number of people of colour could be found working in the mines of south Wales.

Quite what their experience was is difficult to know. This was an era of deep beliefs in racial hierarchies which, despite pseudo-scientific justifications, ultimately came down to seeing lightness of skin colour as an indicator of civilisation. Of course, most people in Wales had no contact at all with anyone of colour but that does not mean they did not share the racisms of the period. Images of Empire were all around, from advertisements for tea to films and children's books and all helped perpetuate ideas of the barbarity of those who were not white. But personal interaction could temper that and reveal a common humanity. In the Cardiff docks, there was widespread intermarriage between sailors of colour and Welsh women and the whole area was a multicultural melting pot that was relatively harmonious most of the time. Onlookers, however, were often disgusted at the interracial relationships and condemned the whole area for its supposed moral failings, violence and crime. It was difficult for anyone of colour to find work or lodgings in other parts of the city. In 1919 race riots erupted in Barry, Cardiff and Newport. The backdrop was economic tension surrounding the problems some returning soldiers faced in finding work and housing but they revealed a racist undertone to Welsh society. Black individuals and their families were targeted by large, angry white crowds that gathered after individual fights had broken out. Shots were fired, the windows of people of colour smashed, their houses emptied, and their furniture burnt. There was serious violence over several nights and three people were killed. In the court cases and newspaper discussion afterwards, there was talk of the need for segregation and even of removing people of colour altogether. When these riots are considered alongside early twentieth-century incidents of Welsh rioting against the Irish, Chinese and Jews, it is difficult not to conclude that industrial Wales was a society shot through with racial assumptions and prejudices.

Education and the decline of Welsh

Racial violence is clear evidence of how Wales was assimilated into British imperialist mindsets. Yet Wales remained culturally different to the rest of Britain because until the end of the nineteenth century the majority of Welsh people spoke Welsh. Indeed, at the beginning of serious industrialisation in the late eighteenth century probably at least ninety percent of Welsh people lived their lives through the medium of that language. Welsh survived conquest, union and then assimilation because the state never tried to prevent it being spoken and actually supported it through sponsoring the translation of the Bible into Welsh. By the end of the eighteenth century, the gentry had largely become English speaking, but they too did nothing adverse about the language their tenants spoke. Welsh was also protected by geography. Wales may have been politically assimilated into England but its mountains limited communication and movement eastwards as much as they did between north and south. The population incursion was limited to the border areas and the planted populations of the medieval period became Welsh speaking over time. Before the railways, most of Wales was relatively cut off from England and that helped keep Welsh alive.

When railways were built, they brought economic benefits to rural communities but also English ways, tourists, and employers. The cultural and physical isolation of the rural north and west came to an end and that inevitably increased the English language's penetration of rural Wales. Industrialisation was a mixed bag for the language too. At first it helped. Unlike in Scotland or Ireland, speakers of the indigenous language could move to other places that spoke that tongue to find better paid work. Only in time did industry bring in migrants from England in numbers large enough to undermine Wales' linguistic situation.

Whereas the first English migrants into the coalfield had learned Welsh, the growing number changed the dynamics of communities with remarkably little tension or outcry.

A small handful of non-Welsh speakers in a conversation in a pub or at work might be expected to make do but as their number increased linguistic dynamics changed. Gradually, it was the Welsh who learned English rather than the English migrants who learned Welsh. This was more than just a matter of numbers. English was the language of education, of the state, of much of the press and popular entertainment. Even some chapels were switching over to it. A Welshman or woman had much to gain from learning English, whereas increasingly the English migrant had little to gain from learning Welsh now he or she was no longer such a small minority.

At the 1891 census, the first time anyone actually counted, 54.4 percent of the Welsh population spoke Welsh, and 30.3 percent only Welsh, although that figure may have been exaggerated by people misunderstanding the question asked. A decade later, the proportion of Welsh speakers was 49.9 percent and the percentage of Welsh monoglots a mere 15.1 percent. Two decades later, population growth meant there were now more than 977,000 Welsh speakers but they only represented 43.5 percent of the population. There were still 190,292 Welsh monoglots in 1911 but they now formed just 8.7 percent of the population. The impact of immigration was evident in how the most dramatic fall was in the coalfield. The percentage of the population of Glamorgan who spoke Welsh fell from forty-nine percent in 1891 to thirty-eight percent twenty years later.

For those who believed that the Welsh language was the soul of the Welsh nation this was more than just the fading of a language. The decline of Welsh remains an emotive subject and blaming it on English oppression is often an attractive interpretation today. The Welsh Not provides some supporting evidence for this and claims that Welsh was beaten out of people's ancestors are today very common.

The Welsh Not's form and name varied from place to place; more commonly, it was known as the Welsh Note and sometimes the Welsh stick. It was normally a small piece of wood that was given to a child who was heard speaking Welsh. If someone else was caught speaking Welsh it was then passed to them. Whoever had it at the end of the morning or day was kept back, made to write out lines or given a physical punishment. Another version was to make a child stand on a bench or on one leg in a corner with the board in his or her mouth until someone else spoke Welsh. Sometimes everyone who had held the Welsh Not that day was punished. One observer recorded that to get rid of the board, the holder would draw fellow pupils into prolonged conversations designed to tax their English. If that failed, they might pinch them to extort a cry in Welsh. Whatever exact form it took, it must have had a psychological rather than just a physical effect and it lies behind the popular claim today that the language was beaten out of the Welsh. However, the reality was far more complex and the Welsh Not is actually a powerful indicator of how far Welsh assimilation into Britain went and the Welsh people's lack of concern at this.

Today, understanding of the Welsh Not has been confused by and mixed up with knowledge of the 'Blue Books'. This was an official 1847 report into Welsh education that provoked outrage in Wales. Its central message was that the Welsh language was holding the Welsh back from civilisation and there were also some derisive accompanying comments on Welsh morality. As one of the most infamous passages put it: 'The Welsh language is a vast drawback to Wales, and a manifold barrier to the moral progress and commercial prosperity of the people. It is not easy to over-estimate its evil effects.' Such passages are sometimes quoted today as an example of English colonialism but at the time these linguistic comments were not particularly controversial. This was an era when the Welsh saw English as the language of progress and a majority shared the view of the commissioners that the purpose of education in Wales should be to teach English. The reports did generate outrage but this centred on the comments on Welsh morality and religion rather than language.

The report has created the idea that the British state was concerned by the impact of the Welsh language but it comes from a period when education was not even compulsory and it did not lead to any state action, let alone any new policies. Instead, before 1870, education was largely the realm of charities, religious bodies and private individuals. Despite its extensive survey of these different types of schools, the Blue Books report actually makes just one reference to the Welsh Not. It came from Llandyrnog in Denbighshire and the reporting commissioner was not impressed with its effect on either learning English or on the behaviour of children.

The single passing reference to the Welsh Not suggests it was not in widespread use in the middle of the nineteenth century but this does not change the fact that it did exist. The earliest written record of anything similar seems to come from Caersws in the 1790s where it was called the Welsh lump, a piece of lead fixed around the neck with string. In that case, the source mentions no other punishment beyond wearing it but school logbooks and autobiographical writing from people who attended schools in the middle of the nineteenth century further illustrate its existence, even if quantifying quite how widespread it was is impossible. The most famous, but probably exaggerated, example is from the patriotic school inspector Owen M. Edwards (1858-1920), who claimed to have received a thrashing hundreds of times for speaking Welsh in school. Like Edwards' account, what is noticeable about the known examples is that the majority come from the middle of the nineteenth century, before the state became closely involved in education.

The Welsh Not also has to be understood in the context of a very harsh education system where physical punishment was used to enforce obedience, manners, and religion. One man who attended a school in Denbighshire in the 1850s remembered that his teacher was cruel and would hit children for speaking Welsh but also anything from whispering, to getting sums wrong, to turning around in class. Like the cane hung on the wall, the Welsh Not may also have partly functioned as a visual tool to ensure children knew not to speak Welsh rather than by being actually passed around. Nonetheless, this does not change its insidious effects. In 1911, a teacher looking back at the practice recorded, 'It will be observed that the system was admirably calculated to destroy self-respect and to foster duplicity and cowardice. In most cases, it simply caused the children to detest the schools and all connected with them.' He was not wrong.

The Welsh Not was never government policy. The 1870 Education Act, which essentially founded state education in England and Wales, made no mention of what language instruction should take place in. It was not even compulsory for children to attend school until 1880. For most of the nineteenth century, the state did not offer any instruction on how teaching should take place. Even after 1870, there were prescribed subjects but what happened in the classroom was up to the teacher and the school board, while schools themselves came under the jurisdiction of local authorities not central government. From 1863, the central state did however offer schools grants based on their students' performance in linguistic and arithmetical skills. Since these results affected teachers' salaries, there have been claims that this led to more use of the Welsh Not. It certainly cemented the place of English in Welsh schools but the wider evidence, nevertheless, suggests that the Welsh Not was in decline after the middle of the nineteenth century. By the late nineteenth century, contemporaries were speaking of it as a curiosity from the past.

Growing state involvement in education actually encouraged more enlightened views towards teaching. There was a move away from constant physical punishments and a greater appreciation of the need for children to understand things rather than just recite them. This encouraged the use of Welsh by teachers and by inspectors who tested the pupils' understanding. Thus from 1875 pupils were supposed to be allowed to answer questions from school inspectors in Welsh. Any teacher wanting to properly teach or control monoglot children properly would have to speak Welsh to them. With children often not hearing any English outside the classroom, immersing them in the language inside the classroom with no explanation of the words they were hearing would simply not work. As a Caernarfonshire teacher noted in 1885, 'nothing but a parrot-like knowledge of English can possibly be imparted to scholars in Welsh-spoken districts ... without freely using the Welsh language'.

That teacher was responding to an enquiry by the Honourable Society of Cymmrodorion which was seeking to establish Welsh as a subject in its own right. The pressure paid off and in the 1890s the Board of Education approved Welsh as an optional subject for schools, although it did nothing to facilitate or support this development. Some schools were already doing this. In 1888, Bangor and Caernarfon school boards, for example, adopted Welsh as a specific subject. In 1897, Welsh was made compulsory in all infant schools in the Rhondda, although implementing this proved difficult because not all teachers spoke Welsh. A Welsh Department of the Board of Education was created in 1907, an important example of how aspects of government were actually devolved nearly a century before the foundation of the National Assembly. The Board became an enthusiastic proponent of offering children a distinctively Welsh education. A 1915 pamphlet it issued, for example, declared 'A good knowledge of Welsh is a thing to be proud of and all Welsh children should praise their Mother Tongue.'

Yet whatever the state was encouraging, things in the classroom could be quite different. In 1885, one Glamorganshire teacher claimed that inspectors were not allowing children to answer their questions in Welsh, even though the regulations permitted this. He concluded 'The great majority of the inspectors are rank Englishmen, whose hobby is to stamp out the Welsh language altogether'. Perhaps more common was a lack of support for teaching Welsh from those who controlled education at a local level. Schools were run by local authorities and school boards and these were now mostly under the control of Welsh Liberals who were very sympathetic to the idea of a Welsh nation. Yet only a few chose to use their power to promote Welsh and it was at this local level that the barriers to Welsh were strongest. Some school boards, inspectors and teachers reminded staff to keep to English as the main language of instruction.

Such attitudes meant that in some state schools, especially in the north, children were still being punished for speaking Welsh in class and in the playground, and that could involve a Welsh Not. In 1875, for example, the school log book for Bryngwran (Anglesey) recorded, 'The children of this school have been of late too much in the practice of speaking Welsh. To-day a rule was laid down that no child in the three upper standards was to speak Welsh during school hours, and that any violate of this rule was to be duly punished. The culprit was found out by means of a "Welsh mark".' However, what the punishment was is not recorded. Given the decline in physical punishment in schools after 1870, it is quite possible that the schools still using, or even introducing, some form of

Welsh Not were not giving beatings for infringements. In this example, it is also notable that it was only for older children, which again illustrates the growing realisation of the need to use Welsh to teach English. But, nonetheless, as this case shows, children in state schools could be punished for speaking Welsh, while the need for punishments shows children were not always speaking English willingly.

Excluding Welsh from the classroom was not state policy, and nor was it controversial. Moreover, it was actually parents who were often driving the practice. They were certainly not seeking to stop their children speaking Welsh but they did want them to learn English. The Blue Books report, like other investigations into nineteenth-century Welsh education, found repeated evidence that the working class wanted their children to learn English and that this was their main motivation for sending them to school. One Blue Books commissioner put this down to money: 'They find an ignorance of English a constant and almost insurmountable obstacle to their advancement in life, especially to their efforts to place their children out at service'. Moreover, as the Blue Books and later investigations again found, parents were actually hostile to their children being taught Welsh at school because their children could already speak the language and could go to Sunday school to learn to read and write it. With English being the language of the state, a global empire and business, it was not surprising that many parents wanted their children to learn the language. Even in the countryside, people could see that those with the better paid non-manual jobs spoke English. Because schools relied on the fees of parents, they had no choice but to follow their wishes and to focus education on learning English. Fees for school attendance were not abolished until 1891, despite attendance being made compulsory from 1880. Parents simply wanted what often drives Welsh-medium education today, a desire for their children to be bilingual so they could get on in life.

The state thus did not try to stamp out the use of Welsh in schools and the decline of the language cannot be blamed on it. Instead, the responsibility lies closer to home with the councils, school boards, teachers and parents who insisted that Welsh had no place in the classroom. But, as the century progressed, such attitudes did become less common and Welsh was increasingly used in the classroom as a means of teaching English more effectively. Moreover, many teachers recognised that punishing children for speaking Welsh did not actually work in helping them with their English. Some schools thus tried different approaches, with one in Llangefni giving out prizes to children who did not speak Welsh. The Honourable Society of Cymmrodorion's 1885 survey of Welsh headteachers found that three hundred and thirty-nine were in favour of Welsh being a specific subject in schools, whereas two hundred and fifty-seven opposed the idea. The main reason given for opposition was the desire of parents to see their children learn English and the teachers' feeling that that the best way to achieve this was to discourage the use of Welsh. This did not mean they were hostile to Welsh *per se*. 'Of course we all love the old tongue, but school life is not a matter of sentiment, but a serious preparation for the battle of life' wrote one Anglesey headmaster in 1885.

The love of the language and the limitations of the influence of education were evident in how, in the countryside, Welsh remained the language of home and of religion. Whatever did or did not happen in schools, at the start of the twentieth century there were still large chunks of the countryside in the west where ninety percent of people spoke Welsh and a third of the population did not speak English. In 1901, as much as forty-eight percent of the population of Anglesey recorded themselves as unable to speak English. Of course, the figure was highest amongst the elderly but across Wales 15.8 percent of three to fourteen year olds were recorded at that year's census as only able to speak Welsh. Even for fifteen to twenty-four year olds, the figure was 10.4 percent. Neither figure was a ringing endorsement of schools' ability to teach English.

Schools may not have stopped children speaking Welsh but they added to the general sense that it was English that mattered and education was a key instrument in the assimilation of Wales. Even the growing use of Welsh in the classroom did not change this since the primary reason was to improve the teaching of English. Schools also encouraged a sense of British patriotism in Wales, just as they did in England. Children were taught *God Save the Queen* or *King* and to take pride in the Empire. They learned English history and stories that celebrated English valour and heroes. Yet even this is not straightforward because the Welsh also often tended to use England and Britain as synonymous terms. Thus, it is not necessarily the case that the children saw these tales as nothing to do with them but rather that they were part of their national inheritance. Moreover, there was the potential for individual teachers and schools to promote Welshness and the existence of Welsh history textbooks is one indication that at least some schools were nurturing a sense of Welsh identity amongst pupils. But there is little to suggest that this was a common occurrence and where it did happen it was not at the expense of Britishness.

In 1885, some teachers claimed that teaching Welsh as a distinct subject would put an end to the 'false shame' many children felt about their language. The roots of this went much further than the classroom. The 1847 Blue Books enquiry had been devastating in its assessment of the Welsh language, which it argued was incapable of being used for modern discourse and was keeping the Welsh in ignorance and away from civilisation. They were not alone in their assessment and it formed a strand of a much wider set of Victorian thinking that regarded Welsh as a relic of the past and unable to articulate modern ideas. When added to the fact that English was the language of commerce, business and education, it was not surprising that many chose not to pass the language onto their children. This was rare in rural areas but once the linguistic balance began to tip in urban areas it became relatively common. At times, the push even came from children themselves. The writer Jack Jones recalled of his childhood in Merthyr in the 1880s: 'The Welsh were in a minority in Tai-Harry-Blawd, where they mixed with English, Irish and Scottish people ... At first I only knew Welsh from my parents and grandparents, but as I went on playing with Scott, Hartley, Ward and McGill children, I became more fluent than in my native language. Dad was annoyed when I started replying in English to what he had said in Welsh, but our mam said in Welsh: 'Oh, let him alone. What odds anyway?'

This was an era dominated by ideas of economic, cultural and scientific progress and English was the language of modernity and of an emerging mass culture. The late nineteenth century saw not just the growth of education but also a shared commercial culture of leisure and entertainment. The growing disposable incomes brought about by industrialisation facilitated the rise of spectator sport, seaside trips, brass bands and male voice choirs, nights at the music hall, fish and chips, cheap novels, local and national newspapers, and, in time, the cinema. Some historians argue that this was a culture of consolation in which the workers found a solace and dignity that was denied to them in a deeply unequal world. As a result, it helped ensure that Britain lacked the political radicalism that capitalism's inequities might otherwise have created. Other historians maintain it helped promote a sense of class consciousness by creating a common lifestyle that transcended regional boundaries and that this helped underpin the growth of the Labour Party.

Whichever interpretation is right, the growth of a mass commercial culture was part of the assimilation of Wales into Britain. For children and adults alike, English was more appealing because it was the language of fun, of penny dreadfuls, comics, the cinema, and radio. It was the language of not just England but of America too. In short, it was glamorous. In contrast, Welsh was the language of grandparents, the countryside and dull chapels. These dynamics did more harm to Welsh than anything the state did or did not do. Welsh was injured not by device but by apathy, economics and fashion. Michael D. Jones, the founder of Patagonia was blunt in his 1894 assessment of this: it 'is the Welsh themselves who are letting English in, and making an effort to turn Welsh out of their families, chapels and trade ... It is up to the Welsh themselves as to whether Welsh dies or lives, and if it dies the blame will be theirs.' This may sound unpalatable, but it may well be true.

A British nation

The question of Wales' assimilation is complicated by the issue of what Wales was being assimilated into and whether there was any deliberate state policy to assimilate Wales. The Tudor state certainly legislated to make Wales part of England for all legal purposes but it also supported the Welsh language rather than tried to eradicate it. In the centuries that followed, that assumption that Wales was part of England for legal and political purposes remained and was cemented in law in 1746 by legislation that declared that any act of parliament that had or would in the future refer to England also applied to the 'Dominion of Wales' and Berwick-upon-Tweed. This Act was not controversial because it was simply making sure of something that everyone assumed was already the case. Instead, it was rooted in the complexities brought about by the union of England and Scotland, a union that did not merge the nations legally or administratively.

What the union of first England and Scotland and then Ireland did do was open the door to a new kind of Britishness. That was a concept which the Welsh had little difficulty buying into since it was by nature multinational and not at odds with Wales' broad understanding of its own history. The state continued to make little effort to enforce this identity on the peoples of Wales, although the gradual emergence of state education did do something akin to that, even if that was not centrally directed. There was actually little need for the state to promote the assimilation of Wales into the new British state because economics and culture were already doing precisely that. Buying into Britishness gave the Welsh of different classes access to markets, jobs and capital. It was also increasingly a source of dignity since it put Wales at the heart of a global power. Coal and metal meant that Wales moved from the economic periphery of the British state to becoming one of its most important centres. It sucked in people and capital from elsewhere. The resulting wealth was not fairly shared out but that was true of every English region too and the result of capitalism not colonialism. When in the early twentieth century the British state sent troops to Tonypandy, Llanelli and elsewhere to deal with a new wave of strikes and industrial unrest, they were attempting to contain the politics of class not nationhood. Meanwhile, beyond the world of politics, a new mass culture had emerged based on the music hall, seaside trips, sport, cheap books and newspapers. In some ways this culture was as much American as British, but it was still part of Wales' assimilation into a popular Britishness through its promotion of the English language.

Karl Marx argued that people made their own decisions but not in conditions of their own making. Welsh people were making conscious decisions about which language to speak but they were doing so in wider cultural, economic and political conditions that pushed them in a particular direction. It could even be argued that the Welsh acceptance of Britishness was the result of a psychological mindset created by conquest and colonisation, where people had been conditioned into thinking their culture and language were inferior. This does accord with thinkers who have discussed colonialism in Africa and elsewhere. The Algerian Frantz Fanon, for example, argued that for colonised people the sense of being uncivilised and inferior was internalised and subconscious. For Fanon, the first stage of liberation from this was to realise it was true.

In Wales' case, it is difficult to disprove or prove what is, ultimately, a speculative idea. But it does seem to take agency away from ordinary Welshmen and women. It suggests that the people who thought themselves British, who were happy to accept the political status quo and the assimilation of Wales, were somehow duped, experiencing what could be called a false consciousness. It certainly overlooks how for many of the Welsh, Britishness was not something imposed on them by the English in order to buy cooperation or accept subjugation. It was a real feeling and a national inheritance even. This sense of Britishness was why the Acts of Union were so readily accepted. It was also a Britishness laden with a sense of moral superiority over others. Just as the Normans had thought conquering the uncivilised Welsh was God's will, so, too, did the Welsh think that the British Empire was right and moral.

The application of ideas like Fanon's to modern Wales is also problematic because Algeria and post-Tudor Wales are radically different. No one was killed or massacred simply because they were Welsh. In other parts of the world, British imperial administrators were enslaving people, shipping food out of starving communities, shooting those who protested their governance, and taking control of lands that did not belong to them. The medieval Welsh had suffered similar fates but now their descendants were taking part in such activities rather than being the victims of them. The Welsh were slave owners not slaves. Even the masses benefited from slavery and the economic exploitation the British state inflicted on the rest of the world. Unlike the Algerians, the Welsh followed the same religion as their conquerors and had the same legal and political rights. They may have spoken a different language but, more importantly, most had the same skin colour. As Britain gained an Empire and began to rule peoples whose appearance and beliefs seemed profoundly different, the cultural variations within its own islands seemed less important than they had before.

Some of the English did, however, still look down upon Wales and the union was not one of equals. This was only too evident in the Blue Books which contrasted Wales' barbarity with England's enlightened civilisation. Even evidence it received from within Wales could make a similar point. A clergyman from Builth declared the Welsh were 'very dirty' and 'more deceitful than the English', while another from Brecon claimed they were, like the Irish, 'dirty, indolent, [and] bigoted'. The Welsh felt judged, abused and condemned. This was probably something limited to the educated classes who read the reports, or at least read about them, but there were casual encounters with the English that reinforced such ideas.

William Abraham was laughed at in 1892 when he switched into Welsh during a speech at the House of Commons, although fellow MPs were probably embarrassed when he revealed he had been saying the Lord's Prayer. Tourists, officials and employers too could pass sneering judgements. And, of course, there were the schools, which even if they did not beat children for speaking Welsh, still left no one in any doubt about which language was the superior. This might all be regarded as cultural imperialism, but it did not make Wales a colony in any traditional sense. Nonetheless, whatever we call it, these attitudes existed, and they left a mark on Wales.

The common cause between Wales and England, and the unequal nature of that relationship was apparent during the First World War. Its outbreak was met with a mixture of apprehension and flag waving. Now we know what was to come, it is easy to dismiss the support for the war as naive, but it was born from a sense of not so much British superiority but a feeling that Britain, and thus Wales too, was in real danger from a barbaric and evil Germanic threat. Some two hundred and eighty thousand Welshmen served in the forces in that war. Some did so because they conscripted or felt duty bound, others were drawn more by the chance of adventure than duty, but Welsh responses were also rooted in a very real British patriotism. To dismiss this as some form of false consciousness or the result of a mind-washing education system would be to insult the intelligence of those involved.

Yet that was also what some officers seemed to do when they encountered soldiers with little or no English, struggling after having been removed from Welsh-speaking communities and thrust into a war being administered and fought primarily through another language. Even understanding marching orders and distinguishing between left and right could be challenging at first. Nor were soldiers always even permitted to write home in their mother tongue since all letters had to be censored. This was more than just inconvenient since not all parents could read English and thus understand the letters their children had sent. Indeed, the same was true of letters sent home by the War Office and thus some parents had to rely on neighbours or others to find out if a telegram was informing them of the injury or death of their son. But official regulations did allow letters to be written in Welsh and the language to be spoken in the trenches, and thousands of soldiers did both. The suppression and sneering thus once again owed more to individual officers and officials than policy but it still created a powerful sense of anger amongst the victims. One father thus wrote to a newspaper: 'If Welsh blood is good enough to be spilt on the plains of Flanders the Welsh language is good enough to be written'.

The war also produced the most powerful argument against post-Tudor Wales being a colony in any traditional sense. In 1916, the same year the Irish were taking up arms against the British, David Lloyd George, a Welsh-speaking Welshman, became prime minister. It is a very odd colony that gets to govern its master during a time of war and crisis. Moreover, he achieved this without abandoning his Welshness. At the outset of war, he summoned the idea of a Welsh military tradition stretching back into medieval times in order to raise support for the war. He also fought successfully to allow Nonconformist chaplains in the army and for the formation of a Welsh division to serve in France.

But Lloyd George's career also shows the continuing inequalities within the union. As a Welshman and a Nonconformist, Lloyd George was always regarded by the British establishment as an outsider and he was frequently sneered at by his political rivals for his background. His Welshness did not stop him reaching the top of politics' greasy pole but it did not make his rise or his ascendancy easy. From the Acts of Union to the present day, the Welsh and Wales have often been looked down upon by many over the border. In any political sense there may not have been a colonial relationship but in a cultural sense there was an inequality that might be described in such terms. Yet the survival of the Welsh language and a sense of history meant Welsh identity survived Wales' assimilation. Indeed, from the late nineteenth century, it underwent a revival and reformation. It is to that story that the next section now turns.

III

Re-creation

In 1886, Basil Jones, the bishop of St David's, remarked that Wales was little more than 'a geographic expression'. In this he revealed how out of touch Anglicans could be with what was happening in Wales. Conquest, annexation and centuries of assimilation had not destroyed Welsh identity. In many ways, this is the most remarkable feature of Welsh history. The resilience of Wales is certainly an idea that is much celebrated. This is evident in the huge popularity of Dafydd Iwan's 1983 song 'Yma o Hyd', which declares that, despite everyone and everything, the Welsh are still here.

But this perspective suggests that Welsh identity has been a rather static concept, whereas it has actually undergone repeated processes of reinvention and redefinition. At the end of the nineteenth century, this happened again and Wales was once more recreated, despite its assimilation into Britain. In this, it was not unique. The nineteenth century was a great period of nation building across Europe. As in other nations, the Welsh 're-creation' was a selective process and involved more than a touch of invention and sleight of hand in choosing what Wales meant. However, the prefix *re-* matters because Welsh identity was not being conjured out of thin air. It drew on understandings of the past and that put the relationship with England at the heart of what it meant to be Welsh. George Borrow wrote in his 1862 travel book *Wild Wales*, 'All conquered people are suspicious of their conquerors. The English have forgotten that they ever conquered the Welsh, but some ages will elapse before the Welsh forget that the English have conquered them.' This may not have been a daily concern but it did create a sense of insecurity around Welshness and so much of the nineteenth-century re-creation of Wales was based around proving an equality with England.

Whatever their source or meaning, an awareness of how national identities can be made and remade has led historians to think of them as 'imagined communities'. This phrase was coined by Benedict Anderson and is meant to convey how nations are based on their members feeling a sense of belonging to them and imagining that they have something in common with the other members. This make nations more ideas than facts. It does not mean the common identity is not real but it does focus attention on how the process is selective and on how different nations imagine themselves as nations for different reasons. Furthermore, the idea of nations as imagined communities highlights how a nation might not hold the same meaning for everyone within it. Just because a group of people think of themselves as a nation does not mean that what individuals imagine is precisely the same. Thus political, economic, social and cultural unity is not a requisite for a nation, as long as there is something to give people some sense of unity.

Such perspectives helped explain why a sense of Welshness survived assimilation into the British state. Since nationality had no fixed rules, it was easy for a people to still imagine themselves a nation, even in the face of political realities that suggested otherwise. For the imagined community that was nineteenth-century Wales, religion was the key underpinning factor. From it sprang a new generation of confident nation builders, eager to give Wales the symbolic trappings of nationhood. Although the Welsh language – the most important reason for the survival of a sense of Welsh cultural identity – was certainly part of this, it was not at its heart. The doubts about whether the language was modern or civilised enough were still there. Indeed, many nineteenth-century Liberals were happy to envision that the language would one day die a noble death. When, amidst the economic ruins of the interwar depression, modernity seemed to have failed, and the death of Welsh seemed likely, then the language was re-evaluated and put back at the heart of new attempts to recreate Wales. Linguistic decline was compensated for by a growing number of national markers in daily life. As the second half of the twentieth century progressed, the Welsh were increasingly reminded of their Welsh identity by education, the media, road signs and even government. The idea of Welshness became embedded in the physical and emotional infrastructure of Wales. This was just as important as political concerns in bringing about the establishment of devolution in 1999. But the fact that only a quarter of the Welsh population voted for that change also showed that for the majority Welshness was not politicised.

Nonetheless, over two centuries, Wales changed from being home to a people with a loose sense of nationhood based on the past, and a language, to some sort of protonation state. The later stages of that process caused, in intellectual circles at least, arguments about whether nationalism was about ensuring Welsh interests and giving Wales what other nations took for granted, or was creating division and hatred and undermining the multicultural tolerance that was supposed to characterise the UK. This all reflected how Welsh nationality held a variety of different meanings for the modern Welsh. For some, it was a highly charged political concept that trumped all others. But, for others, it was a sentimental feeling best left to sporting contests, or St David's day. For a few, it was a complete irrelevance. Class, language, history and community all played their part in determining such feelings but so too did personality. Wales was a deeply personal idea. This was why the historian Dai Smith famously remarked that Wales was a 'singular noun' but a 'plural experience'. One word can mean many different things.

Liberal Wales

The nineteenth century was an era of nation building. Peoples looked to the past and claimed new identities. Sometimes this was to promote a new political identity from within an existing larger unit, as was happening in the Austro-Hungary Empire. But, at other times, it was to bring together different territories to form a new country. Thus, in Germany and Italy, new states emerged out of wider national sentiments, or rather the political exploitation of those sentiments. Even within existing states, there was a strengthening sense of nationhood as newspapers, education and rising democracy helped forge a common patriotic consciousness across different regions under the same governance. Indeed, some historians have suggested that nations come from states rather than vice versa. In this light, what happened in Germany and Italy was the creation of nations from peoples with something in common rather than the unifying of peoples who already felt themselves a nation.

In Wales, the ingredients for a new nation state were there but they were sparse and perhaps rather stale. Wales had endured centuries of cultural and political assimilation into first England and then Britain. The 1830 abolition of the Court of Great Sessions, the legal system introduced with the Acts of Union, ended the last small remnant of unique Welsh administrative distinction. A sense of being a nation was still there, not least because of the Welsh language and a sense of history, but it was dormant and few saw it as having any political relevance. That was until the publication in 1847 of the 'Blue books', the report into education which maintained the Welsh language shut the Welsh off from civilisation, education and social and economic progress. The report is much misunderstood. As the previous section argued, its derogatory comments on the Welsh language were not the focus of controversy in Wales. It tends to be now forgotten how the report also showed an appreciation that Welsh was used in Sunday schools to impart spiritual and biblical knowledge. The Welsh are not dismissed as an inferior race in the way British colonialists looked down on those who were not white. Instead, Wales' problems are treated as cultural. One passage concluded: 'If the Welsh people were well educated, and received the same attention and care which have been bestowed on others, they would in all probability assume a high rank among civilised communities'.

The level of detail in the three lengthy volumes that made up the report implies a vigorous interest in Wales by the British state, but more representative is what happened after their publication in England, which was, at least in government circles, not a lot. London journals, however, dwelt upon some brief passages that made wild and salacious assumptions about the promiscuity of the Welsh, and particularly Welsh women. These sections, and the general English sense of difference and superiority that runs through the reports, have led them to be described as some form of cultural imperialism. That was not how they were seen at the time but the accusations that Welsh women were sexually promiscuous, that the Welsh as a whole were deceitful, and the implications that somehow this was all to do with Nonconformism, were taken as national affronts and there was considerable outrage in Welsh middle-class circles. Insulted, the nation seemed to spring into life. Amidst the outcries, there were attempts to show that the Welsh were more respectable and devout than the English. Illegitimacy statistics were employed to dispel ideas about Welsh sex lives, while crime was often blamed on aliens and outsiders. Thus began a reinvention of Wales by pushing to the fore the idea that the Welsh were a religious, devout and virtuous nation. Once again, the measure for this was comparisons with the English.

At the heart of these arguments was Nonconformism, the combination of religious sects which had come to dominate much of Welsh religion from the late eighteenth century. Since the Blue Book commissioners had relied on testimony from Anglican priests for some of their more outlandish comments, the reports helped create a view of the Anglican church as an institution alien to Wales. It was Nonconformist writers who pushed this idea but they were pushing at an open door. Anglicanism was already the religion of landlords and the upper classes, whereas the people were overwhelmingly Nonconformist. The movement of people from the countryside to new industrial areas reinforced Nonconformism's grip and the new towns boasted what now seems a rather bewildering mass of different chapels. By the middle of the nineteenth century, there were enough chapels pews in Wales to seat half the population. At a religious census in 1851, four out of five religious attendances were by Nonconformists, although many of these turnouts were probably the same people attending more than one service.

Nonconformism was a visible sign of difference to England and it was soon being claimed as the very defining feature of Wales. If religion defined the nation then the accusations of the Blue Books would seem even more misleading but this motive does not mean the Nonconformists were not making their case in good faith. Indeed, so influential were such ideas that by 1891 even former Prime Minister W. E. Gladstone was declaring that 'nonconformists of Wales are the people of Wales'. The power of the chapels also helped ensure the Welsh language had some status in a world where it was often looked down upon. If a language was good enough to speak to God in then it cannot have been all bad. Yet Welsh was never made into a political or social cause by chapel leaders. Instead, they rallied against the tithes and burial laws and the other privileges the church enjoyed. The tithes were taxes the Church of England was able to impose on parishioners whether they attended that place of worship or not. These were not popular in England either, but in Wales resentment was stoked by the sense they were benefiting not just someone else's church but another nation's. In the 1880s resentment of tithes turned violent because the incomes of those having to pay the taxes were under pressure in an agricultural recession. The response in England to the tithe riots was again to see Wales as an alien place. In 1887, *The Spectator* seethed: 'Wales must learn that as long as she is part of England, and shares in the benefits of the English connection, English individuals and English corporations are not to be deprived of their property because the income of that property is not spent in the particular locality from which it is derived.'

In contrast to Anglicanism, Nonconformism appeared to be a culture rooted in the people and specifically operating in the Welsh interest. But it was nevertheless a fragile base on which to build a nation. On the Sunday of the 1851 religious census, nearly half of Welsh adults did not attend either a chapel or church service. Chapel attendance could be simply instrumental, a way of ensuring work at a quarry or colliery when the local management also worshipped there. It could also be out of habit or a need for social contact. There were doubts within chapels as to whether Wales really was devout and this meant they were not always tolerant places for those who sinned. Certainly, as the nineteenth century progressed, this culture of Nonconformity gave Wales more than a touch of austereness in the eyes of outsiders. It came to dominate musical culture, shifting the focus of eisteddfodau from the pub to the chapel. Teetotalism became one of its central concerns and preachers became moral leaders, sometimes as quick to condemn the lives of the people as to uplift their souls. With Welsh identity being based on such insecure sands, then it became increasingly vulnerable. As the monotony and judgemental morality of the chapels turned some of the young away, their identification with Wales was undermined too. Even the Welsh language became tainted by chapels in some young eyes because it was associated with boring sermons and being told what not to do.

But this is to miss what the chapels did achieve, especially in the era before modern rivals for attention existed. As well as, of course, providing spiritual guidance, purpose and well being, they did everything from run Sunday schools that helped spread Welsh literacy to fostering a vibrant social life and providing seaside trips. Even their religious services could have a touch of theatre about them with their impassioned sermons and elaborate rituals. The chapels also crossed class lines and on their pews sat not just workers, but shopkeepers, professionals and industrialists. Indeed, those pews were often arranged in ways that reflected and respected local hierarchies. This meant that while the chapels may have challenged external authorities, they respected internal community authority. Chapels were thus at the heart of communities, and if nations are built from the bottom up, then the claim that Nonconformism was the basis of Wales was not unreasonable.

From Nonconformism also came a Liberal ascendancy over Welsh politics. Chapels were not above openly persuading people to vote Liberal and encouraging anti-Conservatism through their attacks on Anglicanism. The personal, moral and spiritual appeal of ministers and preachers gave their rhetoric considerable weight in the communities they served. The party promoted itself as the defender of religious freedoms and this won it considerable support in Wales. After the vote was given to some working men in 1867, doubling the Welsh electorate, the 1868 election saw a breakthrough for the party in Wales when it won twenty-three seats, compared with the Conservatives' ten. The election was followed by some seventy evictions of tenants from Tory-owned estates and this cemented the idea that somehow the Conservatives were alien and even anti-Welsh. In contrast, the Liberals began to portray themselves as a Welsh party, representing the religion and interests of the Welsh people. Yet it took British democratic developments before they could take advantage of this and it was the introduction of the secret ballot in 1872 and the granting of the vote to all male heads of household in 1884 that really paved the way for the Liberals' domination of Welsh politics. Although more than forty percent of adult males were still not eligible to vote, the electorate was now full of working men who wanted representatives who better spoke to their interests than the gentlemen MPs of old. Industrialisation and the creation of new urban communities had ripped apart some of the old deference in society and the Liberals were the beneficiaries. In 1885, the party won thirty out of the thirty-four Welsh seats. Wales was now not just a

Nonconformist nation, it was a Liberal one too. Again, this mattered because England was not.

The political impact of all this was to remind the British state that Wales did exist at least. In essence, before the Liberal challenge, the British state had regarded the United Kingdom as being formed of three countries. The Irish were recent and rather alien members, while the Scots were much older and nicer but still different. Wales, in contrast, was, to all intents and purposes, a quirky region of England, even though its people spoke a different language. From the 1880s however, Wales' Liberals had the numbers to make their opinions matter in an era when the two main parties in England were relatively evenly balanced. They drew inspiration from the successes of Ireland in gaining disestablishment and land reform and began to campaign for what they considered as national Welsh causes.

Their first success was the 1881 Sunday Closing (Wales) Act, the first piece of modern legislation to treat Wales differently from England and a move away from the political and legal uniformity brought about by the Acts of Union. This symbolism was significant but it also strengthened the idea that Welsh difference and thus identity was grounded in the narrow realm of religion. There were other Liberal achievements. The 1889 Welsh Intermediate Education Act created county schools that became important sources of social mobility. A University of Wales was formed in 1893 and bound together the existing colleges, which themselves owed much to working-class subscriptions. The creation of a Welsh Board of Education helped dispel the anger at state money being funnelled into Anglican schools. A National Library was created in 1907 and then a National Museum in 1909. The Liberal Party was giving Wales its first modern symbols of nationhood and the imagined community of Wales was coming to life. In Cardiff a civic centre was built to home some of these institutions. It also contained a City Hall with a huge dragon perched on its dome and a gallery of marble statues of heroes from Welsh history, all paid for by a Welsh coal magnate. Nearby was Glamorgan County Hall which had at its front a huge sculpture of muscular miners who looked more like Greek Gods. There was little sign here of any colonised mindset. On the back of a buoyant economy, this was a confident nation.

However, the big cause of the Welsh Liberals was the disestablishment of the church, which meant stripping Anglicanism of its position as the official state religion of Wales. This was about recognising and respecting the national difference of Wales but it was not an easy thing to achieve and, despite the weight of Welsh Liberal votes, it was never a priority for any Liberal government. A series of bills got nowhere until 1914, when war disrupted one at its final hurdles. By the time disestablishment finally happened in 1920, it seemed a rather outdated issue that no longer stirred the emotions, but for more than a generation before it had been a veritable battle for Welsh nationhood.

Symbolism only went so far. Influenced by similar demands in Ireland, the 1890s saw a home rule movement for Wales emerge within the Liberal Party. Known as Cymru Fydd, it sought to create a Welsh parliament but failed to articulate any clear need for this or to fuse nationalism with the growing working-class consciousness that might have promoted it. It ran into suspicions between the coalfield and rural areas and collapsed after a meeting in Newport in 1896 where David Lloyd George was shouted down, something he blamed on 'Newport Englishmen'. This was more than just the outcome of cultural tensions but also a realisation that it was being within the British Liberal movement that had helped advance Welsh causes. Political separation might have significant symbolic significance but there was nothing of the popular antagonism to British rule that existed in Ireland to make many feel this was particularly important. Instead, most of the Welsh who thought about these things at all were content with their less radical symbols of nationhood.

In the wake of Cymru Fydd's collapse, the most important Welsh Liberals, Lloyd George and Tom Ellis, turned their backs, by and large, on Welsh issues and instead sought to advance their ideals and their careers in a British context. This is a cause of some lament today and there have been academic criticisms that the nineteenth-century Welsh Liberals failed to develop the kind of separatist nationalist movement that was emerging in other parts of Europe. But for most of the Liberals there was no need. They did not regard Britishness as something imposed on Wales but as a part of Wales and key to its national resurgence. This was perhaps evident in how the royalist Prince of Wales' feathers or the harmless leek were the most popular national symbols rather than the fiery Red Dragon of Wales. As the previous section showed, Welsh Britishness was hardly surprising given that this was a time when the Welsh economy was booming and imperialism was at the heart of that. Even Cymru Fydd was only looking for devolution rather than independence. Many today may not be comfortable with the idea of Wales as part of the Empire but at the time Empires were not seen by most as tools of oppression but of enlightenment and progress. Progress was a very powerful Victorian notion and to go against it would have made little sense. Moreover, since the Liberals regarded Wales as a nation defined first and foremost by religion there was simply no need for any political separatism since the British state was able to guarantee Nonconformism's freedoms. This stance may well have been a missed opportunity to deliver devolution and a nation state that was Welsh speaking but that simply was not a concern of any more than a small minority. Instead, they were content with how they had promoted Wales as a Nonconformist Liberal nation, with a distinct identity within a wider British context and the symbols of nationhood to prove it. They had not invented a nation but they had recreated one.

Popular Welshness

Just as in earlier periods, there are questions as to how far this renewed sense of nationhood extended beyond political and intellectual circles in the late nineteenth and early twentieth centuries. As before, daily concerns were inevitably dominated by issues of work, food, family and housing. But, unlike in other periods, education, economic integration and the emergence of a mass consumer culture meant more contact with the English language and English people. This, in turn, must have made people more aware of their distinctive language and its significance. They may have wanted to learn English but many also seemed to have a deep affection for Welsh and a desire to hold on to it, not least because it expressed who they were in a culture and economy that so often denied them any sense of dignity. This was clearest in rural areas where linguistic change was more about the rise of bilingualism rather than the abandonment of Welsh. In the northwest quarrymen liked to say that the stone they cut and quarried did not understand English. The technical language of their industry was Welsh and in the early 1880s over ninety percent of Britain's slate came from north Wales, meaning that workers there had little sense of being part of a wider industrial class. With quarry managers often being English, labour relations and class tensions in the industry became interwoven with linguistic and national feelings. Elsewhere in Wales, sentiments of nationhood had less tangible bases, but it still ran deeper than the Nonconformist Liberal construction of Wales. Wales may not have been a nation-state, but it had a history, a language, borders and many of the symbols that made nationhood more than just a static idea. This may not have often led to much conscious flag waving but it was woven into the fabric of life, an often unconscious identity that was accepted without question.

The base of this was a sense of history, a history that framed Wales and England as distinct from one another. The future Liberal MP Henry Richard wrote in 1866 that the Welsh 'cherished with great tenacity' stories of their heroes. He claimed 'a passionate, and, I fear I must add, a fierce and vindictive patriotism ... was constantly fed by stories, half fact and half fable, transmitted from father to son, of the cruelty and perfidy of their Saxon and Norman oppressors, and of the victories and defeats which had marked their long struggle for independence'. In the nineteenth century, this spirit was now given a more respectable slant and a stronger written means of transmission. Out of the culture of Liberal Nonconformity emerged a vibrant intellectual culture that produced patriotic histories, religious writings, literature and poetry, although sometimes tinged with a hint of superiority or smugness. There was a renewed interest in Arthur, the *Mabinogion*, and anything else that spoke of Welsh antiquity. Owain Glyndŵr became a firm favourite, not just because of his rebellion but as a patriot and statesman. Poems, books and talks about him became popular and all had a patriotic flavour. In 1909, a public talk at Llandeilo by a schoolmaster from the town declared 'although the country had been conquered, and although there were innumerable castles in Wales to keep the Welsh in subjection' it was 'to the glory of Glyndŵr that he, for a time at least, made himself the leader of the Welsh against Saxon tyranny'.

This history was inscribed into the landscape itself. Even in areas in the east where the language had faded as a spoken tongue, there was still a host of Welsh names for fields, hills, villages and towns which signalled to locals and visitors that this was not England. Many of them conjured up legends, heroes, battles and saints that marked the existence of a distinct Welsh culture. In a churchyard in Nevern (Pembrokeshire), for example, a yew tree (with red sap) stood that was said to weep blood until the local castle was ruled by the Welsh again. Such sites helped people imagine and connect to their nation. As the writer E. M. Wilmot-Buxton put it in 1911 'almost every hill and mound in the district, has its legends, its romance, which lives in the hearts of an intensely patriotic and imaginative people, and blends the past and present into one'.

Much of this culture could be found on show at the National Eisteddfod, an originally bilingual festival of poetry and music which emerged in 1860 out of the vibrant pattern of local events that themselves had their roots in the medieval veneration of poetry. It both promoted and drew on ideas of the Welsh as an ancient people with their own culture, particularly in its use of druidic costumes and a ceremony held in a reconstructed stone circle. Despite some financial difficulties, it quickly became something of an established tradition, not least thanks to the fact that there was nothing similar in England, and it is a powerful example of how a recreated Wales was recreating its history for modern times. Eisteddfodau also helped renew the idea of the Welsh as a musical people and the new patriotism of Wales gained a soundtrack too when a father and son from Pontypridd composed 'Hen Wlad fy Nhadau' in 1856, a stirring, patriotic song memorialising those who shed their blood for Welsh freedom and calling for the old language to live on. Although there was no official body to declare it such, it became accepted as the national anthem with remarkable rapidity in the following years. If ever there was such a thing as an invented tradition to sustain nationhood here it was.

As the title of the national anthem conveyed, the images of this nationhood were overwhelmingly male, a reflection of the patriarchal nature of society. A notable exception, however, was the national costume, another invented tradition. At the start of the nineteenth century, many Welsh rural women were wearing tall hats and cloaks. Such fashions had once been common in England but things had long moved on there, making their survival in Wales seem peculiarly Welsh. As part of the plundering and reimagining of the past in the drive for Welsh nationhood, this outdated style was refashioned and turned into a national costume but now with a distinctive red cloak, a petticoat and a bigger hat. The driving force in this was Lady Llanover, the wife of a wealthy Monmouthshire politician, landowner and industrialist. She encouraged its use amongst her servants and at the local eisteddfodau she held. Gradually it became a symbol of nationhood used on postcards, newspaper cartoons, and consumer products. Like Nonconformism in the wake of the Blue Books, it represented a Welshness that was supposed to be homely, moral and even pure, but, unintentionally, it also cemented an English view of the Welsh as a little ridiculous.

Looking back, we can regard such cultural artefacts as recreating Welsh nationhood but that is not how they were seen as the time. The Victorians did not regard their Wales as something being made but something natural and even biological. This was in line with a much wider belief that different nations were based on racial categories. Thus, in and outside Wales, there was a strong sense that the Welsh were a Celtic race. This not only made them different to the English but also gave them a shared, linguistic and cultural inheritance with Scotland and Ireland, although this did not stop the often deep-seated prejudice that existed in Wales towards Irish Catholics. It also meant there was a belief that the Welsh had certain physical characteristics. In the 1880s, John Beddoe carried out a study of the peoples of Britain which argued that while the Welsh were not homogenous, they generally had broad cheekbones, short compact builds and dark complexions. Being part of a Celtic race was also thought to shape the Welsh character too. The Welsh were widely regarded, and indeed regarded themselves as an emotional and sometimes hot-tempered people, something which set them aside from the more sombre and sober English. This was used to help explain their musical talents but it was thought to have political consequences too. Matthew Arnold, a professor of poetry at Oxford, thought the Celts spiritual and sentimental romantics rooted in the past, unsuited to the demands of the world and thus unlikely to survive.

Large-scale immigration into the Welsh coalfields in the late nineteenth and early twentieth century challenged these ideas of nationhood. Although racial definitions of Wales continued to be offered, they made little sense in a world where so many were moving in. Such movements also undermined the chapels, although many switched to the English language in order to protect their hold over communities. Liberalism was another casualty and political debate increasingly shifted from symbolic Welsh issues to how the party was failing the working class. At first, a slow general rise in living standards had doused the fiery radicalism of the Chartists and the Merthyr rising, while the sting had been taken out of rural anger over rent and access to land by the job opportunities that nearby coalfields offered. Yet Wales remained a deeply unequal society, and Liberalism had little to say on that. The political fallout of this was delayed in the coalfield by the party co-operating with working-class leaders who were also committed to Nonconformism and spoke Welsh. For a while, this helped create the idea of a common cause between the Liberals and the working classes but it failed to disguise the fact that the Liberals' national causes were increasingly irrelevant to the majority, who had simpler economic priorities.

A key turning point came in 1898 when one hundred thousand south Wales miners were locked out from work in a dispute over whether their pay should be linked to the price of coal. The result was the formation of the South Wales Miners' Federation, a body that united the workforce against the increasing concentration of coal ownership in large combines rather than small companies. This, like the refusal to continue accepting that wages should fall when the price of coal did, undermined any sense of a shared interest between employers and employees and created a much more oppositional culture in the industry and its communities. Whereas once communities had appeared to be united by language and religion, now they seemed divided by class. From this came calls across industrial Britain for a specific working-class party and in 1900 Scotsman Keir Hardie became

Wales' first specifically Labour MP. His background and rhetoric showed that class was coming to matter more than nation in most people's allegiances, but this did not mean a rejection of Wales. As the Labour movement and party grew in stature, it gradually became seen as a symbol of Wales in itself and the nation regained its reputation for popular radicalism. This was partly because the Labour Party itself was interwoven with the cultural politics of the chapel and was quite happy to embrace and promote the Welsh language.

Any visit to a major sporting venue would have shown that socialism had not killed patriotism. Sport grew with the industrial revolution and, by the end of the nineteenth century, it was firmly established as an integral part of popular culture in industrial communities, despite the disapproval of some Nonconformists. Following the lead of England and Scotland, and in tune with the general culture of national symbolism that was emerging, the Welsh middle classes formed national associations to govern rugby and football. Many of the other symbols of this re-created Welsh nationhood were limited in their appeal but sport had a wider reach than Nonconformity, the Welsh language, the Liberal Party or any of the national institutions that it created. More than that, sport was exciting and laden with its own symbolism. Its teams were named after places, and standing in a large crowd made people feel part of something bigger. Thus rugby in the south and football in the north gave communities that were becoming increasingly diverse through the effects of industrialisation and migration, an accessible and successful banner under which to unite. Clubs and the national sides both enabled immigrants to declare new loyalties, without having to conform to any religious or linguistic idea about what those identities meant. The fact that sport united workers and the middle classes, and was perhaps a distraction from political tensions or even the pub, also helped its popularity amongst the leaders of the new Wales. Rugby's adoption into the mainstream of Welsh culture can be traced by the changing attitude of David Lloyd George. In 1895, he wrote to his wife that the industrial valleys of Monmouthshire were less responsive to his radical politics because their inhabitants were 'sunk into a morbid footballism'. In 1908, he saw his first match and exclaimed 'It's a most extraordinary game ... and I must say I think it's more exciting than politics'. Whether he meant it or not, that he said so publicly suggested that sport was now firmly entrenched in the cultural landscape of Wales.

A key moment in that transformation came in 1905. Before forty-seven thousand at Cardiff Arms Park, New Zealand took on Wales at the end of a successful tour that had seen the tourists defeat England, Ireland and Scotland. Wales triumphed by three points to nil, after New Zealand were controversially disallowed a try. Wales had succeeded where the other home nations had failed and had upheld the honour of the British motherland. Contemporary Welsh writers got rather carried away and saw the match as a moment of glory for not only a triumphant nation but a triumphant race too. Overlooking how some of the team were actually migrants from England, the editorial of the *South Wales Daily News* excitedly declared:

The men – these heroes of many victories that represented Wales embodied the best manhood of the race ... We all know the racial qualities that made Wales supreme on Saturday ... It is admitted she is the most poetic of nations. It is amazing that in the greatest of all popular pastimes she should be equally distinguished ... the great quality of defence and attack in the Welsh race is to be traced to the training of the early period when powerful enemies drove them to their mountain fortresses. There was developed, then, those traits of character that find fruition today. 'Gallant little Wales' has produced sons of strong determination, invincible stamina, resolute, mentally keen, physically sound.

A nation's progress and the racial superiority of the Celt: the press coverage of the victory was indicative of the national confidence and consciousness that abounded amidst the economic and cultural buoyancy of late Victorian and Edwardian Wales. It certainly did not suggest a nation that had been bullied and oppressed into thinking it was a second-class colony.

Across Europe the growth of newspapers and print culture was central to the making of modern nations and, as the coverage of rugby suggested, something similar happened in Wales. The second half of the nineteenth century was a golden age for newspapers and periodicals. Most were in English but Welsh-language publications were seen as ways of stemming the assault of English culture, while English or Welsh Conservative commentators looked at them with suspicion, fearing they were fostering radicalism and agitation. Newspapers were key agents in local identities but many were also consciously Welsh in thought and outlook and they helped fashion a sense of popular and modernised Welshness, especially amongst those who did not speak Welsh. Nor were they modest about their sense of national identity. In 1901, the *Western Mail* went as far as declaring Wales 'one of the brightest and most truly civilised spots in the Queen's dominions'. Although they sometimes articulated linguistic and religious divides, the printed media also brought together north and south, turning the nation's eyes inwards in a way that had never really happened before. It was a key player in the remaking of Wales and a forerunner of what the BBC would do in later years.

Yet both the press and sport also showed how for workers and for the middle class, Welsh patriotism in the late nineteenth and early twentieth centuries still existed squarely within a British context. Welsh newspapers in both languages praised the Empire and royalty, while sport mattered because it enabled Wales to beat England. The Welsh [Rugby] Football Union chose as its symbol the Prince of Wales' three feathers. The co-existence of the two nations was only too visible in 1911 at the investiture of the future Edward VIII as Prince of Wales at Caernarfon castle. This was the brainchild of Lloyd George. In the face of rising class tensions, growing antagonism in Ireland and strains between the Lords and Commons, the royal ceremony was an opportunity to pull the different components of Britain back together whilst still acknowledging national distinctions within it. The ceremony made extensive use of the Welsh language and Welsh iconography such as dragons, daffodils and leeks. Indeed, for some commentators, it represented a final sign that the Welsh had defeated centuries of attempts to extinguish their nationality. As one Welsh-language paper put it, 'we have won the day over the English and have conquered totally their cruel attempt and traditional policy to weaken and destroy Welsh nationality ... We have at last grasped the sword from our enemy and buried it in his own heart.' But it was also a celebration of reconciliation and Wales' place within Britain. The ceremony and many of the discussions of it used the imagery of marriage to depict Wales and the monarchy being tied together. The king himself reminded the audience that his son was descended from the house of Tudor and thus claimed the allegiance of the Welsh. It is tempting to see the investiture as part of a deliberate conspiracy to tie Wales to the British nation. That was certainly part of the investiture's intention and the message of unity in diversity was meant to resonate across the Empire. But the reality was that the message was needed far more beyond Wales. In Wales, it was a reflection of how Welsh patriotism already existed within a British imperial context.

Although the 1911 investiture was well received in England, the new national confidence in Wales did not always appeal much to the English. The old suspicions evident in the Blue Books never disappeared but were now added to by a vague sense that Welsh patriotism was somehow emblematic of a lack of gratitude for how the Union and Empire were helping Wales. In 1912, a supposedly humorous book entitled *Taffy was a Welshman* declared that Wales, like Ireland and to a lesser extent Scotland, was pretending to be a country:

cut off and aloof from England, countries whose noble and superior inhabitants have been basely enslaved by English trickery, and brought to the very depths by English plunder and injustice. Consequently they cry out for ever of their wrongs and woes; they boast for ever of their un-Englishness, and babble for ever of their separateness and independence, and of the importance of their petty languages and extraordinary 'national aspirations.' During the past half-century this vicious and ridiculous spirit has developed to an extent which the Saxon does not altogether appreciate. In Wales especially it is raging and rampant.

More common than seeing the Welsh as a political threat was a tendency to sneer or just laugh at them. The nursery rhyme that began by declaring that 'Taffy was a thief' and ended with the narrator breaking 'Taffy's head' was very well known and appeared in a whole host of children's books, even as late as the early 2000s. Whatever its intensions, it cannot have helped the image or self-esteem of the Welsh. Nor did the widespread use of 'to welsh' or to 'welch' to describe breaking a deal or bet. Well into twentieth century, and even beyond, the Welsh were the subject of musical hall and postcard humour that mocked their language, backwardness and country ways. This may have been typical of wider humour that jested at anyone and anything different, but again it was hardly indicative of a union built on equality. It also had the effect of creating amongst some a sense of embarrassment about being Welsh. Wales could still inspire intense emotional feelings but it could also seem to be rather old-fashioned, something to be played down, especially when confronted by the snobberies of the British class system and its distrust of outsiders. Thus, in 1932, the travel writer H. V. Morton recalled meeting a man in Ruthin who told him: 'When I first went to England I suppose I spoke with a Welsh accent, but it only made people laugh. Paddy and Jock are good fellows, but 'Taffy is a Welshman, Taffy is a thief''. He returned home to Wales.

Yet Wales was actually becoming less distinct, at least in cultural terms, and both English and Welsh views of the nation and its people were misleading. By emphasising what made Wales different, the Welsh were often guilty of imposing stereotypes on themselves. By 1911, just 43.5 percent of the population spoke Welsh. Sixty-two percent of the population lived in the heavily-urbanised counties of Glamorgan and Monmouth and Welsh towns were as modern as anywhere in the world. Many of the Welsh were Conservatives and Anglicans. The upper class, particularly those who owned large estates, were never quite as harsh in their operation of rent and tenancy as either contemporaries or some historians have made out. The Butes, for example, redirected some of their industrial income towards their tenants by providing new buildings and drainage for them. The Anglican church too was not quite the alien institution it was often portrayed as being. Stung by the threat of disestablishment and the charges levelled against it, it had increasingly embraced Welsh culture, invested in new places of worship for its parishes, updated its services and ensured its clergy were more professional. In 1870, it appointed its first Welsh-speaking bishop since the early eighteenth century. By 1910, it was the largest single religious body in Wales and home to over a quarter of all religious attenders. This in many ways typified how the recreated Wales was based on straw men. Emphasising differences to England had helped define a sense of Welshness but they were misleading and, ultimately, they limited the reach and appeal of Welshness amongst those who did not share in its narrow central pillars.

And yet still, the late nineteenth- and early twentieth-century Welsh seemed reluctant to emphasise too much their language, the deepest and most tangible sign of difference to England. There was considerable pride in Welsh but it was of a sentimental and unpoliticised sort and the language was rarely placed centre stage in the new Wales. More often than not it was the language of home and hearth, of the private rather than public sphere. Welsh was a language to sing in, to pray in, even to debate in, but only for a few was it really the heart and soul of the nation. More perhaps, thought, with time, it would fade away.

The re-creations of Wales also papered over the divides that were opening up within the nation. It was not even always clear where Wales actually was. This was only too evident in Monmouthshire. It was excluded from the 1881 Welsh Sunday Closing Act, although a decade later the census showed that its population was fifteen percent Welsh speaking. In 1921 the county was added to the legislation in official acknowledgement that it was Welsh after all, even if not all its residents agreed. Other places went in the opposite direction in a series of minor amendments to the nineteenth-century border brought about by the need to establish to which counties places belonged for tax and administrative purposes. Not everywhere got their wish. In Flintshire, for the Maelor Hundred, a small area protruding into England, an 1880s boundary commission found that a 'great preponderance of opinion exists among all classes' in favour of its transfer into Shropshire. It recommended the transfer of a number of parishes to England but these were not all followed through. Thus Maelor Hundred remained in Wales, despite the apparent wish of its residents to be English.

Language was one of the considerations used in deciding on which side of the border a community should be. The first language census in 1891 revealed just how much levels of Welsh speaking varied across the country. This partly reflected proximity to the English border or, in the case of south Pembrokeshire, medieval settler implantations, but it also showed how industrial immigration was changing the culture of the valleys and opening up a new rift within Wales. In Sir Alfred Zimmern, a politics professor at the university in Aberystwyth, gave some definition to these feelings of division:

> The Wales of today is not a unity. There is not one Wales, there are three ... There is Welsh Wales, there is industrial, or, as I sometimes think of it, American Wales; and there is upper-class or English Wales. These three represent different types and different traditions. They are moving in different directions, and, if they all three survive, they are not likely to re-unite.

North and south was another divide. With rich dialects and distinct accents, different sporting cultures, few transport links and little reason for anyone to visit the other, the two halves of Wales often remained psychologically removed from each other. Yet there remained a deeper sense of Welshness which united the regions and it was religion, culture, the sense of history, and all the national symbols created by the Liberals that underpinned this. Moreover, those who dwelled upon the divides also overlooked how people moved around and how family ties crossed the boundaries, at least within north and south. For example, there were still in the 1920s miners with families on farms in the south-west, who would head there for holidays and even to help with the harvest. All nations have geographic and social divides. These do not undermine nationhood because, ultimately, it is an idea rather than a category which has to adhere to any strict definition that all agree upon. It was this that ensured Welshness prospered despite assimilation but it also meant Welsh identity had little focus or political salience.

The destruction of Wales

Between the two world wars, much of the economy in Wales collapsed. The combination of a global economic downturn, an aging industrial sector in need of modernisation, the loss of overseas markets and the advent of the age of oil all hit Welsh industry and especially coal. With so many communities relying on single heavy industries, the result was devastating. In some places male unemployment hit more than sixty percent. One result was mass emigration and more than four hundred and forty thousand men and women headed off for the greener economic pasture of England and beyond. The industrial depression did not just kill jobs. It also murdered the old vision of Wales, although in this it had accomplices in the influences of mass education, class-based politics, the wireless and cinema. The chapel pews were increasingly empty, the Welsh language continued to decline and the old vibrant confidence of the middle classes evaporated. By the 1931 census, just 36.8 percent of the population spoke Welsh.

There was some renewed talk of a need for devolution but few blamed the English or system of governance for Wales' economic woes. Instead capitalism was seen as the enemy and there was a shared sense of suffering with the unemployed of industrial Scotland, England, Europe and beyond. Class consciousness had intensified, something helped by the shared experience of war. Salvation was thus generally sought in a socialist Britain. The Labour movement dominated Welsh politics, fighting hard at a local level to protect people from the worst of public spending cuts and the effects of unemployment.

However, a small minority of intellectuals thought otherwise, especially as it became evident that the numbers speaking Welsh were in serious decline. For the first time, abating this became a serious political cause. In 1925, a small group formed Plaid Genedlaethol Cymru, Wales' first nationalist party. Faced with the crisis of language and economy, they began to look for what they thought was the real, authentic Wales. Their focus was not on the industrial towns but the countryside which many of the inhabitants of those towns had left behind. It was here that the gwerin, the idealised, cultured, intelligent, Welsh-speaking people, were to be found. They were not entirely the stuff of fiction but what the gwerin did offer nationalists was a vision of Wales that was reassuringly divorced from the realities of modern society. In many ways, the emerging nationalist movement was about preserving a rural culture rather than fostering the Welsh nation as a whole. Indeed, it echoed contemporary feelings in England where some intellectuals and romantics worried about the loss of traditional customs, dialects and regional distinctions. But what made things different in Wales was the sense that modernisation was threatening the very existence of the nation. Thus while people in England might bemoan the loss of green spaces to housing or reservoirs, they did not think the nation itself was in danger. In Wales, some people did because for them the coalfield and towns were not part of Wales. For romantic nationalists in Wales, the nation was the countryside, its people and their language and all seemed under threat from the forces of modern society, whether that was through the allure of jobs in English towns or proposals to flood the landscape, as in the Ceiriog valley in the 1920s.

The Second World War intensified those feelings as tracts of land were requisitioned for use by the military. The most controversial came at Mynydd Epynt in Breconshire where two hundred and nineteen people lost their homes when the War Office requisitioned forty thousand acres in what a chapel minister described as a conscious attempt to 'destroy our nationality'. The loss of land was not the only fear the war raised amongst nationalists. Plaid Cymru complained that the 'English government' did not have the right to conscript Welshmen. Not many shared this view or concern, and the

government did, in theory at least, allow Welsh nationalism as grounds for conscientious objection. More
commonly, there was resentment amongst nationalists
about the influx of English people, not so much at an individual level but in terms of their collective impact. Thus
civil servants, soldiers, broadcasters and even child
evacuees were all seen as agents of anglicisation.

Welsh nationalists made up a tiny proportion of the
population and the Second World War is often thought of
as a time when Britishness peaked. Propaganda, bombing,
the threat of invasion, the shared sacrifices of serving in
the armed forces and enduring rationing all created a
common sense of purpose amongst the British people,
bringing together its different nations and regions. That
sense of solidarity also seemed to cut across gender and
class lines in a war where everyone was 'in it' together.
This was a feeling that the state was only too keen to
encourage and it helped ensure that the news and popular
entertainment were dominated by such messages. Yet the
idea of a united Britain was not straightforward. There
was no single notion of a British national identity.
Tensions were rife and Britishness was subject to different
meanings; it was read and constructed differently by
different regions, sexes, races and classes.

The plurality of British identity meant that a sense of
Welshness was neither lost nor subsumed during this
period of heightened Britishness. More contact with
England made people more aware of not just what they
had in common but also their differences, especially in the
context of a war that was being fought over issues of
national identity and self-determination. With national

identity being discussed in pubs, papers, pulpits and pro-
grammes on the radio, it is unsurprising that at least some
of Wales reflected on what it meant to be Welsh. For parts
of the Labour movement, there were fears that unless
there was stronger Welsh representation in London government there would be a return to the economic
catastrophe of the depression. For probably many more,
national identity was just a simple pride in where they
were from, something that was only inflamed when
ignored or not recognised.

The government was aware of that and, to avoid undermining the war effort, it made efforts to ensure Welsh
nationality was recognised. In 1942, legislation was
passed giving people the right to speak Welsh in court.
Two years later, there was the first ever House of
Commons debate set aside specifically for Welsh issues.
The BBC was reminded not to say England when it meant
Britain and there was a general push for propaganda that
displayed the plurality of Britain. This did not mean there
were not tensions and the odd civil servant or military
official who did not understand or recognise Welsh difference. There were thus complaints that soldiers were being
prevented from writing home in Welsh, despite this being
officially allowed. But this was about the implementation
of policy, not its formulation. It is not unreasonable to
conclude that there was a greater sensitivity to Welsh
identity in London government during the Second World
War than there had been at any previous time.

The tensions between Welshness and Britishness which
rose to the surface during the war laid the basis for future
trends. The economic and political reconstruction of the

1940s reflected practical rather than cultural considerations and Wales was rather overlooked in bureaucratic arrangements. There were Welsh 'regional' boards for health, gas and town and country planning but not coal, electricity, the Post Office and the railways. There were vocal complaints from politicians that there should be more of a Welsh dimension to planning and policy. W. H. Mainwaring, the Labour MP for Rhondda East, argued in 1946: 'There is a growing conviction that, in present government circles, Wales does not count as a nation, that at best it is a province of England'. There was thus clear support among many Welsh MPs for a Secretary of State for Wales, not because the post would be a symbol of Welsh nationhood but rather because it would help prioritise Welsh needs within government. However, the Labour government was unwilling to consider it. Herbert Morrison, the Deputy Prime Minister, suggested that a Welsh Secretary of State would lead to overly complex government administration, negate efficient central planning and suffer from a lack of competent Welsh civil servants. With the war now over, there appeared to be little need for the government to take Welsh sentiment seriously.

Welsh demands were diluted by internal dissent. The Ebbw Vale MP Aneurin Bevan, in particular, was a formidable opponent to anyone who advocated any form of separate Welsh policy. At the 1944 'Welsh day' at the House of Commons he had spoken against the idea that there were uniquely Welsh problems or solutions, and asked how the problem of rearing sheep on Welsh mountains differed from the problem of rearing them on

Scottish mountains. Bevan's antipathy was mixed up with a degree of unease about what role the Welsh language might play in government. In 1946, he told the Commons of a fear in some of the English-speaking parts of Wales of 'a vast majority tyrannised over by a few Welsh speaking people in Cardiganshire' and of 'the vast majority of Welshmen' being 'denied participation in the government of their own country'.

Bevan and others also had a powerful sense of solidarity with the wider British labour movement, a sense that was epitomised by the South Wales Miners' Federation voting in 1945 to dissolve itself and become part of the new National Union of Mineworkers. It was Britain that had won the war and it was on a British scale that the majority of people felt that reconstruction needed to happen. The nationalised industries, the unions and the welfare state thus became part of what historian Linda Colley has called the 'mundane architecture of Britishness'. They symbolised the British nation and people's popular attachment to it, adding to the popularity of the British media, the memory of the war, and a popular pride in royalty. These were all, by and large, tangible realities in people's lives. Moreover, the migration of the inter-war years, where nearly half a million people left Wales, and the continued attraction of England to the socially and economically ambitious after the war, meant that family ties increasingly spread beyond Wales. Thus, as Welsh nationalists were only too aware, the economic and social transformations of British life in the middle of the century were further tying Wales into the British system. Indeed, Britishness itself was actually intensifying as the Empire gradually dissolved and continental European nations came together without the UK. This meant a reduced sense of the British nations as part of international systems and instead newspapers, politicians and others developed and spoke of the idea of Britain as a place apart. Without an Empire or even a place at the fore of international politics, Britishness became a rather defensive identity to be promoted at almost any opportunity. As a result, 'Buy British', for example, was a message heard as often in Wales as in England.

For most people, the wider worlds of Wales, Britain and the globe formed a background to more prosaic concerns and being Welsh, like being British, was a 'given', obscured somewhere amid the noise of daily life. For those who spoke Welsh, this was less true because their daily life often revealed how the language and its associated culture were in decline. But the resulting sense of Welshness was still a diffuse and unfocussed sentiment that found life in a loose sense of difference to England. The minority who were nationalists, however, despaired. They felt economics and politics represented a form of cultural imperialism, oppressing Wales without ever being open about it. They lamented how unfocussed Welsh identity was and how some Welsh speakers were raising their children in English in order to help their future prospects. The young themselves increasingly associated Welsh with the old and stuffy chapels, and it had little appeal in an Americanised modern world of rock'n'roll. But it was not just the working classes of the industrial south who were losing the Welsh language. In rural areas too there were falling numbers of Welsh speakers. In

Caernarfonshire, for example, the percentage of people who spoke Welsh fell from eighty-six percent in 1911 to sixty-eight percent in 1961. In rural areas and industrial districts west of Swansea, much of the working class may still have spoken Welsh but they did not politicise its use. This meant that there was the danger that, as the number of Welsh-speakers in communities declined, those who could still speak the language might find it easier to switch to English in all aspects of daily life and the disintegration of Welsh-speaking Wales would be complete.

Yet that unfocussed Welsh sentiment could be aroused, just as it had been by the Blue Books a century before. In the 1950s Liverpool planned to build a reservoir in the valley of Tryweryn. This meant the flooding of a marshy landscape and the removal of six farms and the village of Capel Celyn, with its forty residents, school, chapel, burial ground and post office. The villagers claimed they found out about the plans only when surveyors arrived there. Throughout the process, the local authority in Liverpool seemed dismissive, and even callous, towards the residents whose homes it was destroying. They were naturally upset but the scheme angered many others too. A Welsh-speaking community was being destroyed to provide water for an English city that seemed deeply reluctant to discuss it with the people whose homes it was taking. It was easy to see the project as another piece of the English imperialism that was killing the Welsh language and way of life. Iorwerth Peate, a prominent nationalist and curator of traditional Welsh life, claimed the flooding was part of the 'gradual murder of the Welsh national personality by various forces from beyond the Dyke'.

The minister responsible for Welsh affairs during the parliamentary bill's first stages was Gwilym Lloyd George. That Wales was being despoiled by the Welsh-speaking son of perhaps its greatest national figure deepened the anger. One letter he received trusted he would 'not sell Wales and be a traitor'. A Wrexham preacher just asked, 'I wonder what your father would say about it?' A letter from Swansea summed up the dominant tone of the complaints received by the government: 'We in Wales are fighting to the last ditch to defend our language and our culture. We dread to think that a power like Liverpool Corporation has the freedom to walk into our country and steal our water and our land in this tyrannical way.' The natural beauty of the area, the question of human rights and the economic future of Wales were also recurring themes and many of the complainants stressed that they were not nationalists. In a forgotten dimension to the affair, many trade union branches also voiced their opposition. It took place against a backdrop of rising unemployment and there was much concern that the transfer of water to Liverpool would hamper future industrial development in north Wales, perhaps by attracting companies to Merseyside that might have otherwise come to Wales, had the reservoir's resources been kept there. But even such fears, though not motivated by concern for the Welsh language or the community being drowned, were still understood within the context of Welsh resources being taken by England. Indeed, for all those not personally affected, the key issue was the fact that the flooding was being imposed on Wales and that awoke the normally unfocussed sense of popular Welshness. One woman told a journalist that she would not have minded so much had the water stayed in Wales 'but it's all going to England, don't you understand?' But in Parliament few English politicians seemed to give much weight to arguments based on either the rights of individuals or Welsh culture. They preferred to look at what they thought was the collective British good.

At the Liverpool Corporation bill's first reading, thirty-five of the thirty-six Welsh MPs voted against it. David Llewellyn, a Cardiff Conservative and the only Welsh MP in favour of the measure, argued that opponents did 'an ill service to Welsh culture by suggesting that its survival depends on sub-standard houses, a dog-in-the-manger attitude to untapped resources, and a callous indifference to the prosperity of Merseyside, where there are far more Welshmen than in the whole of Merioneth'. Yet opposition in Wales was neither as widespread nor as sustained as is often made out. Campaigners claimed that only three percent of people in the Bala area had refused to sign the petition. One English reporter wrote this was because Welsh politeness meant no one liked to say 'no' when asked to sign. He said he was told in private that many would be disappointed if the lake was not built because construction workers and then visitors would bring money to an area of high unemployment. Plaid Cymru certainly worried that its campaign was meeting with apathy. Bala Town Council itself declined to support it, while Merioneth County Council did so only on a second vote and then it was a close decision. As the legislation passed through Parliament, opposition petered out. Only twenty-seven Welsh MPs voted against its second reading. By the third reading just twenty voted in opposition. Denbighshire County Council and other organisations withdrew their objections, leaving Merioneth County Council and a parish council as the only formal objectors.

One man who had farmed in the valley for over fifty years wrote to the government: 'So much is said about this Valley by people who do not know anything about the place'. He complained that many of the members of the Capel Celyn defence committee were outsiders and Plaid Cymru members who did not know the conditions that locals had been living in. Whether this farmer represented local views is unclear but it shows that the community was not united in outright opposition. The government was also told by a local trade union representative and justice of the peace that 'many of those affected by the dam did not really regret it, but did not like to say so in view of the pressure from the Nationalists'. By 1957 Gwynfor Evans was informed by an adviser that 'the vast majority' of Tryweryn residents were 'more than satisfied' with the compensation and were 'satisfied for the scheme to proceed'.

There was ten years between the scheme being announced and the opening of the reservoir. It was a long, drawn out and stressful process for the people of Capel Celyn. Children grew up with it hanging over them. Residents moved away at different times, with their homes being demolished once they were empty. They did go to nearby housing more modern than in the un-electrified village they were leaving behind, but they were given little help in finding new accommodation. The last residents to leave had had to watch their community being literally knocked down around them.

A second re-birth

What the affair did show was how Welsh demands could easily be outvoted if they clashed with English interests. With just five percent of the UK population, this was inevitable, and it was in this that the inequity of the union really lay rather than any deliberate English colonialism. But government also had a duty to ensure minorities were not entirely forgotten and it wanted to avoid any controversy, no matter how marginal. Unsure whether the furore over Tryweryn represented a wider suppressed sense of nationalism that could flower in the right conditions, successive governments set about trying to acknowledge Welsh interests.

This process had actually begun before Tryweryn. Decolonisation across European empires had raised questions about national sovereignty and national rights, whereas the growth of the state led to questions in political and intellectual circles about whether it was attentive enough to Welsh issues. In 1951, 'Welsh Affairs' was added to the portfolio of the Home Secretary by a new Conservative government that was looking for ways to make inroads into Labour territory. In 1954, the government began giving financial support to the publishing of Welsh-language schoolbooks, and in 1959 new legislation allowed local authorities to support financially the National Eisteddfod. In 1958, a new steel development went to Llanwern rather than Scotland, after anger in Wales that the construction of the Forth Bridge had been given priority over a bridge across the Severn. Cardiff was made the official capital of Wales in 1955 and four years later the Red Dragon was declared the official national flag. Rural Welsh sentiment was also protected when a new law to allow referendums on discontinuing Sunday pub closing required them to be held at county rather than at an all-Wales level. These Conservative concessions may have been symbolic and the result of external pressure on the party but they also show how the existence of a minister for Wales and then sensitivity over Tryweryn increased the influence of Welsh interests in government. Yet the Conservatives refused to create a Secretary of State for Wales, arguing in private that the country was too small, did not have its own legal system and would not be best served by an expensive separate administration.

In contrast, internal pressure from Labour MPs led that party to finally commit itself to creating a Welsh Office and Secretary of State for Wales, a promise which it honoured when it returned to power in 1964. Welsh government, even if primarily by civil servants, was now a reality. Not everyone in Labour was enamoured, betraying how so many in the party had a narrow view of Britishness. In his diary, minister Richard Crossman called the Welsh Office an 'idiotic creation' and 'completely artificial'. But one immediate benefit was felt. The new department took the importance of expanding the M4 far more seriously than the Ministry of Transport had done and plans were quickly put in place for a series of new sections. Three years later, the 1746 Wales and Berwick Act, which declared that Wales was always to be included in every new English law unless otherwise stated, was repealed. Henceforth England did not automatically also mean Wales when it came to legal and legislative matters.

In many ways, these actions were enough. There was simply no widespread demand for anything more substantive, but nationalism was an emotive cause that could find a political outlet when combined with economic concerns and an emerging culture of standing up to authority. This is what happened in Carmarthen in 1966 when Gwynfor Evans became Plaid Cymru's first MP. It was partly a protest vote but also a watershed moment that marked the beginning of separatist nationalism as a serious political force in Wales. Before 1966, Plaid Cymru had been a marginal voice in Welsh politics but concern at the falling number of Welsh speakers – who had declined to twenty-six percent of the population by 1961 – was creating new demands for Welsh rights, especially in the rural communities where the language was strongest. There were rumblings of dissatisfaction with the Labour hegemony in English-speaking industrial Wales too. By-elections in Rhondda West (1967) and Caerphilly (1968) saw Plaid Cymru nearly topple mammoth Labour majorities as people voiced their concern at the loss of mining jobs. But it was the politicised student generation of the 1960s who seemed most attracted to radical Welsh issues, particularly the question of language rights. Inspired by the US civil rights movement and its tactics, they, alongside some older similarly-minded people, occupied public places, refused to pay taxes demanded only in English, and vandalised or removed English-only signs.

Knowing the youth protests had wide support amongst older Welsh speakers, the reaction of the government was the 1967 Welsh Language Act which gave the nation's two languages equal validity and stated that provision should be made to facilitate the use of Welsh in official and public business. But how this was to be achieved was not outlined, making the act more symbolic than practical. Thus direct action intensified and campaigners used the legislation to support their calls for bilingualism in public life. Gradually, concessions were made and more public forms and signage became bilingual, with the effect of creating a visual public reminder of how Welsh culture was different to England. But this only happened because people were willing to campaign and break the law for it.

Others were willing to go further. At the start of the 1950s, led by a Swansea barrister, a group called the Welsh Republican Movement broke away from Plaid Cymru. They were suspected by MI5 of having firearms, explosives and links with the Communist Party. Most of their action was limited to burning Union Jacks but in 1952 they tried to blow up an aqueduct and a member was convicted of possessing explosives. Tryweryn caused others to turn to such tactics and explosives were used to attack the construction site in 1962. At the reservoir's opening was a group of uniformed young men calling themselves the Free Wales Army. Over the course of the 1960s, they not only paraded in public but also made outlandish claims about their numbers, equipment and readiness to wage a violent guerrilla war. It was mostly just bluff but their claims ended up convicting six of them in a politicised trial in 1969. Far more serious was a small group known as Mudiad Amddiffyn Cymru who planted a series of bombs around Wales in the late 1960s.

To try to calm things by awakening people's sense of Britishness, the Labour government held an investiture for the Prince of Wales at Caernarfon. It was a lavish affair, awash with Welsh and British pageantry and a touch of celebrity culture based around the young prince. The majority of the Welsh people seemed to either enjoy or ignore it but for a minority the flames of resistance were stoked. Young people held sit-ins and demonstrations; they complained that the event was a political stunt, a colonial imposition and a waste of public money. To offset the criticism, Charles was sent to learn Welsh at university at Aberystwyth, where he turned out to be rather popular and said sympathetic things about the Welsh cause. Indeed, Charles's determination to recognise the national question worried George Thomas, the Secretary of State for Wales, enough for him to write to the prime minister voicing his fears that the Prince had come under too much nationalist influence at university. He suggested the Queen have a quiet word with her son. For the day of the investiture, Mudiad Amddiffyn Cymru planned four bombs. At Caernarfon, two members were killed on the previous day when the gelignite they were carrying exploded. On the day itself, another bomb exploded harmlessly near the garden of the chief constable of Gwynedd. Four days later, a ten-year-old holidaymaker lost a foot after tripping on explosives planted in an ironmonger's yard which Charles had earlier passed. Another bomb was left on Llandudno pier but failed to explode. Later that year, two men were arrested; they went on to be sentenced to ten and six years in prison for their part in the bombing campaign.

Not many agreed with the method but the violence did ensure Wales could not be ignored by government. The calls of the moderates, for more political and language rights, now had more weight because they could be seen as concessions that would avoid the more sinister violence on the horizon. Demands were also bolstered by a more pronounced sense of Welshness in many other walks of life. Rugby, enjoying a golden age on the pitch, became particularly virulent in its expressions of national sentiment in the 1970s. The language itself began to be seen as more modern. It became a medium for pop music, sex and other icons of the age, freeing it from its associations with the old-fashioned chapel culture that was in its death throes. One result was a growth in Welsh-medium education and adult education classes in English-speaking areas. Even what Wales meant was being redefined. As traditional industries slipped into terminal decline, they began to be considered as part of Welsh history and heritage. Working-class culture was now being celebrated as having a clear Welsh dimension. As Plaid Cymru targeted this, the Labour government began to realise the dynamics of the UK were changing and in danger of slipping beyond its control.

Its biggest fears lay in Scotland. There nationalist sentiments were also growing and had the added support of the discovery of North Sea oil which made the proposition of some form of self-government seem far more feasible. Growing demands for this, together with Labour's fear of losing support in its Scottish and Welsh bases, very suddenly made devolution a mainstream political topic in the 1970s. As in the nineteenth century, a political situation in England, where there was little between the two main parties in their levels of support, gave weight to the political demands of the other British nations. The outcome was the 1979 devolution referendums in the two nations. There was little enthusiasm for it in the Labour government but it was a way of placating nationalist sentiments that could otherwise easily escalate into demand for independence.

The referendum gave Wales the opportunity to shake off the English 'shackles' in a meaningful and political way, but the Welsh voters gave the idea a resounding 'No'. At the end of a decade where Welsh rugby had suggested a confident, even aggressive national identity, only 11.8 per cent of the electorate voted in favour of the creation of a Welsh assembly. There were regional variations but even in Gwynedd, the area with the highest proportion of Welsh speakers, less than a third of votes cast were for Yes. The pro-devolution campaign had failed to communicate its vision and suffered from a wider climate of economic problems and distrust of the Labour Party's record in national and local government. But the vote was not just about practical politics. It was also unavoidably about nationality. The emergence of the Northern Irish troubles had not helped since it associated so-called 'Celtic' nationalism with extremism and conflict. The 'No' campaign consistently played upon fears that devolution would mean the English-speaking majority being ruled by a Welsh-speaking clique from the north and that it would ultimately lead to the breakup of the UK. 'Keep Wales united with Britain', declared a full-page advert from the 'No' campaign in most of the Welsh papers on the day of the vote. After the result, a cartoon on the front page of the *South Wales Echo* showed a woman sitting down with a map of Britain on her wall, saying, 'There's lovely – still in one piece'. Determining precisely why people vote in a certain way is impossible but it is difficult to avoid the conclusion that the 1979 referendum also marked the majority of the Welsh asserting their satisfaction with remaining within the United Kingdom.

Later in 1979, Margaret Thatcher became prime minister, after a general election that saw the Conservatives win a third of the Welsh vote. In office, Thatcher became hated in Wales in a way that no previous prime minister had. Much of this centred on her perceived role in the huge decline in the manufacturing sector, the loss of thousands of jobs in the steel industry and the near ending of the Welsh coal industry. In many ways, industrial decline dated back into the 1920s, with the growth of the 1950s being a blip in a long-term trend. More immediately, the collapse in manufacturing was rooted in a wider recession that predated 1979. So, too, was the winding down of publicly-owned heavy industry. But, whereas the previous Labour administration had played down what it was doing, Thatcher seemed to revel in it. This helped create the idea that somehow her policies were deliberately targeting the Welsh, although she received similar reactions in deindustrialising areas of England too. Some of her policies and rhetoric about unions, public waste and private housing were actually quite popular but her period in office helped broaden the idea that the British state was broken and marginalising Welsh interests.

Partly to compensate for the scale of economic upheaval, Thatcher's government enacted a number of changes that did much – indeed more than any previous government – to buttress the fortunes and status of the Welsh language. After Plaid Cymru leader Gwynfor Evans threatened to starve himself to death, the government agreed to create a Welsh-language television channel. It also increased the subsidies to Welsh-language services and gave the language a place on every schoolchild's timetable. The powers of the Welsh Office were extended and a host of new Welsh quangos were set up to monitor and govern Thatcher's free-market state. With quangos being appointed rather than elected, and control of the Welsh Office being decided by how England voted, little of this was very democratic. But it did help modern Wales become a more defined and official nation than ever before and administrative devolution reached such proportions that it was not misleading to talk of the emergence of a Welsh state.

Such developments put Welsh devolution back on the agenda. There was little popular pressure for this but in academic and political circles it was seen as a way of ensuring democratic control over the new Welsh institutions and mitigating the effects of being governed from London by a party for which Wales had not voted. Such demands were far stronger in Scotland and that ensured that when the Labour Party returned to power in 1997 it enacted new referendums on the question of devolution. Wales this time voted by a margin of less than seven thousand votes to enact its first ever degree of democratic national self-government. The imagined community was now something resembling a democratic state creating, in theory at least, a civic Wales based on residency and political citizenship. And yet only half of the electorate had voted in the 1997 referendum. Just one in four of the electorate had supported the most radical change in Welsh politics since the Acts of Union.

Nonetheless, it was a significant shift from the 1979 referendum. The highest levels of support came in Welsh-speaking districts but the key change from two decades before seemed to be amongst working-class voters in industrial areas. It may be that this was the result of Welsh identities becoming more important, filling a void created by class fading in its emotional hold over people due to social mobility and the decline of traditional industries. At the same time, some of the key pillars of Britishness – the nationalised industries, trade unions, the memory of the Second World War and the popularity of the Royal Family – were also losing their grip on the popular imagination. In their place, Welshness was now more evident in everyday life than it had been in 1979. The Welsh media has been growing since the 1960s and, particularly at sporting events, the BBC, HTV and Welsh newspapers could be very patriotic. The education system was also pushing 'Welshness' more, with all children now having to learn Welsh and attention to Welsh issues a curricular requirement in other subjects. From arts councils to economic development bodies, there were new national institutions to add to the traditional sporting ones, and their control over much of public life was significant. The National Assembly was simply a democratic executive to control an administrative devolution that had already taken place. This all happened at a time when so many of the traditional pillars of Wales were wavering in the winds of social and political change or even being blown away altogether. Whereas once Wales had been defined by Liberalism, socialism, Nonconformism, the mines and the Welsh language, now it was somewhere defined by institutions that in effect said 'here is a nation'. Most of all, this mattered because none of those defining features had ever encompassed the whole population of Wales and all were now in retreat. But now the imagined community was something more tangible: a nation with an administrative structure that touched everyone's lives.

In theory, this should have meant the relationship with England mattered less but those institutions still had to operate within a political framework dominated by decisions made in England. Even at a popular level a widespread sense of Britishness remained. The figures for those expressing a British identity might vary across Wales, with it being lower in the western rural areas where the Welsh language was strongest, but nowhere was there evidence of a widespread rejection. This was because so much of daily life – the realm where people understood who they were – was no different in Wales than in England. The Welsh and English spent the same money and shopped in the same chain stores. Youth culture was a powerful shared experience where national distinctions were mere window dressing in a broader pattern of music, clubbing, drinking and partying. Most importantly, Welsh people of all ages read the same newspapers and watched much the same television as the rest of Britain, despite the growth in Welsh programming. English-medium television, like the press, assumed and developed a common identity, speaking to the audience as fellow Britons and situating them within a national calendar and culture. As it had done since the 1950s, it generated shared hopes and fears, interests and outlooks. If Wales was a colony, television was a far more active agent of this than any government. The legal system and the welfare state were important too, although maybe less so than in the past, as their reputations were jaded by scandal on the one hand and familiarity on the other. Finally, England remained very close, both physically and psychologically. People moved back and forth over the border for entertainment, work and education. At the 1991 census, a fifth of the Welsh population had been born in England. In this light, just one in four of the Welsh electorate voting for devolution was hardly surprising. Nor was the lack of support for independence.

This Britishness, whether it was a conscious identity or just an inevitable part of culture in an assimilated nation, may have undermined politicised Welshness but it did not stop Wales mattering. Despite the large scale migration from England, for a majority of the Welsh, regardless of their gender or colour, Wales remained a central part of how they saw themselves. They might not have agreed about what that meant but through songs, goals, land-scapes, and the like, its pull could be very emotional. Some bemoaned that this feeling did not go further, that people were not willing to translate it into a movement for independence. Indeed, some Welsh nationalists saw the cultural hold of London over the media, the allure English jobs held for the young, and the movement of English people into Welsh-speaking communities as forms of colonialism, chipping away at Welsh identity and culture. These did have very real impacts on Welshness and the Welsh language but they were not happening because anyone was consciously trying to eradicate Wales or exert a hold on the country. This means colonialism is not the right word to describe what were outcomes of an unbalanced economy and political union. Moreover, to say any of this was a problem was to privilege one understanding of Wales over others. In reality, the very strength of Welsh identity, and the very reason for its resilience, was how it could mean many different things all at once. Being part of Britain, or indeed Europe, did not change or undermine that.

Wales and the union

In 1945, Major Sir Goronwy Owen, the Liberal MP for Caernarfonshire, asked the prime minister if 'in view of the fact that the Welsh nation is a distinct nation and, in proportion to its numbers, has contributed as much as the three other constituent nations to the greatness and security of the United Kingdom' that Wales could be represented on the Royal Arms of the UK. He maintained this would be 'a very graceful gesture' to a nation that 'played its part so nobly during this war and during every war, and has always shown its loyalty to the Crown and to the Government of this country'. His question summed up the dominant Welsh identity from the late nineteenth century. It was, for most, a distinct nation that existed within another nation. It was loyal to that other country and eager for a recognition that was not always forthcoming. The prime minister replied to Owen that the case needed careful consideration but the Royal Arms remained unchanged, with England, Scotland and Ireland represented on it but not Wales.

Yet Welsh identity was never straightforward. It meant different things to different people and was constantly evolving. In the late nineteenth century, on the back of economic buoyancy and anger at English disdain, Welshness was recreated around Nonconformism, Liberalism and a series of national institutions. In the face of economic problems, socialism replaced Liberalism as its defining political characteristic. But, in time, this too diminished, as did the place of religion in Welshness. For a few, a new vision of an independent Wales emerged but more commonly Welsh identity became a civic concept, based not on class or culture but on living in Wales and being subject to the jurisdiction of the Assembly, its government and a host of other national institutions. The Welsh language was always important, and it became more political as its decline quickened, but this made some feel excluded and it opened a rift in Welsh identity. Sport, on the other hand, was not political, did not raise awkward questions but did offer opportunities to beat the English or at least remind them of Wales' existence. It thus became a cornerstone of popular Welshness. There were times when a lack of confidence characterised the nation but there were other times when Welsh culture was exuberant to the point of arrogance, at least when the economy was booming before the First World War. Whether confident or fragile, Welsh identity survived because people wanted it to. In the face of assimilation, Wales could easily have died away. Just as nations are created, they can be uncreated. But the Welsh chose to be a nation.

The tangled, slow burning outcome of the reinvention of Victorian Welsh identity was devolution. Neither were about opposing Wales' status within the United Kingdom but both assumed Wales was different to England and were about ensuring Welsh interests were recognised by the British state. Neither was born from the assumption that Wales was a colony but both realised that in a large polity it was easily marginalised. Making up roughly five percent of the UK population, Wales was never going to be a major player in British state affairs. Between the arrival of full democracy in 1928 and devolution in 1997, only in four general elections did how Wales had voted make any difference to the overall result. Only in eight of the eighteen elections did Wales end up with government by the party for which it had voted. The dynamics of a political union, where one nation dwarfed the other three, was inevitably going to be dominated by the larger member. The English rarely thought of Wales unless it impinged on national politics in some way or threatened political unrest. Wales was simply not big enough to matter much at a UK level. There was no attempt to destroy Welsh culture, language, or identity but Wales was never a priority for the British state either. This was a geographical, demographic and economic imbalance but it was not colonialism in any traditional sense.

However, when the numbers stacked up, as they did in the late Victorian period, a Welsh group of MPs could be influential and push for what they wanted. Even when parliamentary numbers did not benefit Wales, a democracy still required voices to be listened to and Welsh interests were not entirely marginalised. But this did not achieve enough or go far enough for some, and direct action and violence also played their part in getting Welsh interests noticed and listened to. This worked because it seemed to be a tip of an iceberg. Behind those willing to break the law for their nation were thousands of others who were sympathetic to their cause. It was through various combinations of these pressures that significant concessions were made to Wales. The church was devolved, the pubs were shut on Sundays, Welsh was allowed in courts, Wales was given representation at cabinet and an official capital and flag, the Welsh language received financial support, public bilingualism became the norm, Welsh was taught to every schoolchild, and significant powers devolved to a new self-governing body.

Some would argue that these developments were not about helping Wales but about keeping it within the union. If this is the case, then colonialism might be a term that has some validity. This does require, however, a rather conspiratorial view of all politicians that always assumes the worst. It also overlooks how it was Welsh politicians enacting some of these changes through their positions in British government. It is further difficult to describe recognitions of specifically Welsh interests as colonialism because it was part of a wider process where the British establishment made concessions when its authority was challenged. It thus gradually extended the vote to the working classes and allowed their representatives into the corridors of power, as long as they contained their demands. Thus radical Welsh and working-class leaders, who might otherwise have brought the establishment down, became part of the very entity they were challenging. It was through this route of compromise and accommodation that democracy, a welfare state and a devolved United Kingdom evolved.

But, intentionally or otherwise, this process also enabled both England and the ruling classes to retain their cultural, economic and political dominance. Friedrich Engels wrote that the English knew 'how to reconcile people of the most diverse races with their rule; the Welsh, who fought tenaciously for their language and culture, have become entirely reconciled with the British Empire'. Certainly, because the modern British state allowed Welsh individuals into its highest echelons and because it recognised Welsh difference rather than tried to stamp it out, it was far easier for the Welsh to accept their place in the union. Thus, throughout the modern period, the state saw off Welsh nationalism through kindness, concession, and inaction. This rather than oppression is the real story of modern Wales. No British government was particularly interested in Wales, even when there were Welsh voices around its cabinet table. For all the periodic concessions to Welsh demands, all British governments were more prone to ignore rather than exploit Wales.

Even if the will had been there, there was no need for governments to take action to suppress Wales since the Welsh as a whole were already loyal to the concept of union and empire. Centuries of assimilation meant most did not see the British state as an alien imposition. They may not have been represented on the Union Jack, but they felt British. It was not imposed on them in any act of colonialism but fused with their Welsh identity, no more distinguishable for the majority than Welshness and a sense of local identity. The lack of desire to break free of Britain was evident in every UK general election since 1900; parties committed to the union always received at least eighty-five percent of the Welsh vote. Nor is there anything to suggest that the English did not regard the Welsh as British. They may not have always been seen as the equals of the English but the Welsh were still accepted and this owed much to how most were white and protestant. For the English, this made the Welsh 'one of us' when compared to the despicable Irish and French Catholics and the uncivilised peoples of different colours. Thus, unlike in Ireland, the British state did not act as an alien imposition in Wales. Had it done so, and been more oppressive, then Welsh nationalism would have been significantly stronger. But Wales was not Ireland. It was sniffed at and ignored rather than actively oppressed, and neither inspires revolt or revolution.

Nonetheless, by the end of the twentieth century, the growing recognition of Wales and the popular commitment of the Welsh to the United Kingdom could not change how the British state was failing Wales. The Welsh language continued to decline, despite its enhanced status. Devolved government was hamstrung by a lack of resources and a lack of powers, although some thought a lack of ideas was more to blame for its lack of impact. As across Britain, people of colour and women earned less on average and found it more difficult to gain positions of political, economic or cultural power. Successive governments failed to deal with the deindustrialisation of Wales. The decline of heavy industry and manufacturing and the growth of a low-paid service sector left Wales the poorest part of the UK and one of the poorest places in western Europe. The problem was not the passing of dirty and dangerous industries but the fact that nothing of substance replaced them. In some ways, devolution made the problem worse. The Welsh government did not have the resources (and possibly the imagination) to do much about Wales' economy, while the British government was no longer entirely responsible for it and thus never made it a policy priority. The net result was inaction and large groups of people who felt angry and marginalised. One outcome was heavy support for Brexit. The same was also true of the deindustrialised regions of England, again suggesting that the primary cause of inequity and marginalisation was not colonialism. For all its inherent imbalances, the UK state failed Wales, not because it was dominated by England, but because it was capitalist.

AFTERWORD

The history of Wales is one in which the nation became more defined in political terms but less distinctive in cultural terms. The political institutions developed at the end of the twentieth century made Wales into a proto-state and gave it more unity than had ever existed before, even in the days before conquest. But this also came at a time when its linguistic, cultural and religious difference to England had faded. Indeed, the development of political institutions owed much to people's desires to hold back or compensate for the changing cultural situation. There was nothing inevitable about any of this. Both cultural and political changes were the outcomes of people's choices. Wales survived and evolved because people wanted it to. The decline of its cultural distinctiveness owed much to people's choices too.

Wales could easily wither away if the Welsh no longer feel it matters. But it might also see its political independence grow too. If that does happen, it will be a product of the historical process of the continual making and re-making of Wales. Yet history offers no clue as to whether this might happen or should happen. It offers no answers to the questions that would need to be answered for independence to succeed. How would five hundred years of political union be unravelled? Can a nation in which a fifth of the population was born outside its border develop a strong enough sense of identity to want to be independent? Would independence solve the inequalities of society?

History has no answers but it does explain why those questions are worth asking. The nation has a heritage that is long and has mattered a great deal to a great many people. It shapes who the Welsh are and the conditions they live in, even if it does not provide a guide to what happens next. History offers Wales everything and nothing.

Wales' history can also make people feel uncomfortable. Historians from England, committed to the survival of the United Kingdom, often seem readier to face atrocities and injustices in every part of the Empire than they are in their nation's first colony. Even historians in Wales can be uncomfortable with exploring the nature of conflict and conquest in medieval Wales. Perhaps they fear that highlighting these things might feed modern nationalisms, racisms and even violence. Yet should we really bury the past and shy away from its less comfortable implications? Those who are comfortable with ideas of Welsh nationalism can feel uncomfortable with Wales' history for different reasons. As the injustices inflicted on medieval Wales drifted beyond living memories, and the nation itself was annexed out of legal existence, the Welsh not only reconciled themselves to their new position as members of a British state but revelled in it. They were no more coerced into Britishness than the medieval kingdom of Gwynedd gave up its independence voluntarily. Wales after the Tudors was simply not a colony of England. This is not a story upon which to build a movement for independence. To ignore this history, and to only concentrate on the examples of English oppression and disdain, might feed Welsh separatism but it would be a partial truth.

Reading the past through the prism of the present is always problematic. Terms such as nations, empires, colonialism, ethnicity and race would not always have made much sense to the Welsh of the past, at least in the ways we use them. They can lead us down analytical alleys that might turn out to be dead ends, or at least detours from the more important main thoroughfares. But they can also be ways of communicating what happened to modern audiences. If modern ideas and modern parallels help our understanding, then they have their place in history.

A similar problem occurs with thinking about the idea of Wales itself. It has not always existed. It has evolved, grown and jumped about. It has been articulated in Welsh, English, Latin and other languages. There are huge leaps of supposition and even guesswork to be made in understanding what people in the past meant by it. But none of this invalidates mapping the idea of Wales back, even into periods when contemporaries did not use it. There is a link between the Wales of today and the Wales of early medieval times and even before. It was from those people that the idea of Wales evolved. They are the ancestors of Wales. To take them out of the story makes no sense.

That story belongs to everyone in Wales, no matter where their family heritage lies and no matter how they understand who they are. Indeed, immigration has been a constant feature of the history of Wales. It is part of the rich diversity that has made Wales what it is. Understanding and appreciating this should help create a more open and inclusive Welsh society today.

But, for that to happen, the history of Wales needs to be told and retold. For a nation whose sense of itself was so often sustained by history, Wales today is sometimes re-markably ambivalent about its history. Its castles are used to attract visitors but are not centres of debates about Welsh identity and the relationship with England. Wales' industrial heritage has become more a matter of nostalgia than a source of anger about the inequality, environmental destruction and human cost it created and extracted. More often than not, Welsh children seem to learn more about the histories of England, Germany and Russia than their own nation. This is surely not right, even if some do fear some nationalist plot in calls for more national history in the schools of Wales. The purpose of teaching Welsh history is not to glorify, celebrate or even perpetuate the nation. It should be about understanding who we are, warts and all. Nonetheless, part of that understanding should be the sense of nationhood that the Welsh have had. That is not something invented by writing or teaching about it. A sense of being Welsh was, and is, a historical fact.

The poet R. S. Thomas once wrote there was no present or future in Wales, only a past. It was a bitter sentiment, born of a dislike for the condition of the nation he lived in. But perhaps that condition came from not understand-ing that past properly, from dwelling too much on the losses, whether political, economic or cultural. Wales needs to also understand what it has not lost: its achievements, its diversity, its complexity, its longevity, its democracy. Wales is no longer a colony. Its people are free to make their own future and their own decisions. They are free to choose to be who they want to be, as individuals, as a col-lective, as a nation. The people of Wales just need to decide what it is they want, and where it is they want to go.

SOURCE OF QUOTATIONS

Page

1   Linda Colley, *Britons: Forging the Nation 1707-1837* (London, 1992), p. 6.

3   Margaret MacMillan, *The Uses and Abuses of History* (London, 2009), p. 68.

5-6   Russell Davies, *Hope and Heartbreak: A Social History of Wales and the Welsh, 1776-1871* (Cardiff, 2005), p. 13.

10   William Glover, *The Little Red History of Wales* (Newport, 1913), pp. 10-11.

24   'bestial': *Gesta Stephani* quoted in John Gillingham, *The English in the Twelfth Century: Imperialism, National Identity and Political Values* (Woodbridge, 2000), p. 11.

26   Rhigyfarch quoted in Robert Bartlett, *The Making of Europe: Conquest, Colonization and Cultural Change, 950-1350* (London, 1993), p. 312.

26   'unbearable tyranny' quoted in R. R. Davies, *The First English Empire: Power and Identities in the British Isles 1093-1343* (Oxford, 2003), p. 5.

29   Orderic Vitalis quoted in Mary John, 'Where are the Flemings?', Pembrokeshire Historical Society (2016). Available online at http://www.pembrokeshirehistoricalsociety.co.uk/where-are-the-flemings/

38-39 Llywelyn ap Gruffudd quoted in Trevor Herbert & Gareth Elwyn Jones (eds), *Edward I and Wales* (Cardiff, 1988), pp. 33-34.

40   Statute of Wales quoted in R. R. Davies, *The First English Empire: Power and Identities in the British Isles 1093-1343* (Oxford, 2003), p. 27.

40   Welsh chronicler quoted in R. R. Davies, *The Age of Conquest* (Oxford, 1987), p. 353.

46   Residents of Caernarfon quoted in John Davies, *A History of Wales* (London, 1993), p. 184.

57   Bishop of St David's quoted in R. R. Davies, *The Age of Conquest* (Oxford, 1987), p. 15.

64   George Owen quoted in J. Gwynfor Jones, *Wales and the Tudor State: Government, Religious Change and the Social Order, 1534-1603* (Cardiff, 1989), p. 32.

66   Text of Acts of Union in Ivor Bowen, *The Statutes of Wales* (London, 1908), pp. 75-93, 101-3.

73-74   William Richards, *Wallography, or, The Britton describ'd being a pleasant relation of a journey into Wales ... and also many choice observables of that countrey and people* (1682).

74   Daniel Defoe, *A Tour Thro' the Whole Island of Great Britain* (1724-27), letters 6 (part 3) & 7 (part 1).

85   *Saturday Review*, 14 August 1869.

85-86   Glamorgan teacher in The Honourable Society of Cymmrodorion, *Enquiry as to the Introduction of Welsh into Elementary Education in Wales* (1885). Appendix to Report, p.17.

89   Michael D. Jones quoted in Lucy Taylor, 'Global perspectives on Welsh Patagonia: the complexities of being both colonizer and colonized', *Journal of Global History*, 13, 3 (2018), 446-68, p. 456.

96   'vast drawback': *Reports of the Commissioners of*

Inquiry into the State of Education in Wales (London, 1848), Part II, p. 309.

97-98   1911 teacher: T. Gwynn Jones, 'Bilingualism in the schools', in *National Union of Teachers Souvenir of Aberystwyth Conference 1911*, p. 249.

99-100   Caernarfonshire and Glamorgan teachers in The Honourable Society of Cymmrodorion, *Enquiry as to the Introduction of Welsh into Elementary Education in Wales* (1885). Appendix to Report, pp. 5, 16.

99   'A good knowledge of Welsh', quoted in Tim Williams, 'The Anglicisation of south Wales', in Raphael Samuel (ed.), *Patriotism: The Making and Unmaking of British National Identity, vol. II: Minorities and Outsiders* (London, 1989), pp. 197-201.

100   Bryngwran school logbook in David A. Pretty, *Two Centuries of Anglesey Schools, 1700-1902* (Llangefni, 1977), p. 210.

101   'ignorance of English': *Reports of the Commissioners of Inquiry into the State of Education in Wales* (London, 1848), Part II, p. 254.

102   Anglesey headmaster in The Honourable Society of Cymmrodorion, *Enquiry as to the Introduction of Welsh into Elementary Education in Wales* (1885). Appendix to Report, p. 3.

104   'false shame': The Honourable Society of Cymmrodorion, *Report of the Committee appointed to Inquire into the Advisability of the Introduction of Welsh into the Course of Elementary Education in Wales* (1885), p. 7.

104-105   Jack Jones, *Unfinished Journey* (London, 1938), p. 22.

106   Michael D. Jones quoted in Tim Williams, 'The
        Anglicisation of south Wales', in Raphael Samuel
        (ed.), *Patriotism: The Making and Unmaking of
        British National Identity, vol. II: Minorities and
        Outsiders* (London, 1989), pp. 197-201.

109   Builth and Brecon clergymen quoted in *Reports of
        the Commissioners of Inquiry into the State of
        Education in Wales* (London, 1848), part II, pp.
        295 and 297.

111   Father quoted in Ifor ap Glyn, "Dear Mother, I am
        very sorry I cannot write to you in Welsh …':
        Censorship and the Welsh language in the First
        World War', in Julian Walker & Christophe Declercq
        (eds), *Languages and the First World War:
        Communicating in a Transnational War* (London,
        2016), pp. 128–41.

113   Basil Jones quoted in Matthew Cragoe, 'Wales', in
        Chris Williams (ed.), *A Companion to Nineteenth-
        Century Britain* (Oxford, 2007), 521-33, p. 521.

114   George Borrow, *Wild Wales: Its People, Language,
        and Scenery* (London, 1872 edition), p. 163.

116   Dai Smith, *A Question for History* (Bridgend, 1999),
        p. 36.

117-118 'If the Welsh people…': *Reports of the
        Commissioners of Inquiry into the State of Education
        in Wales* (London, 1848), part II, p. 313.

119   Gladstone quoted in *The Spectator*, 10 October
        1891.

120   *The Spectator*, 4 June 1887.

125   Lloyd George quoted in Kenneth O. Morgan,
        *Revolution to Devolution: Reflections on Welsh
        Democracy* (Cardiff, 2014), p. 124.

127-128   Henry Richard, *Letters and Essays on Wales* (London, 1884), p. 37.

128   Talk at Llandeilo: *The Welshman*, 12 February 1909.

129   E. M. Wilmot-Buxton, *Peeps at Many Lands: Wales* (1911), p. i.

131   John Beddoe, *The Races of Britain* (London, 1885), p. 260.

134   David Lloyd George quoted in Gareth Williams, *1905 and all that* (Llandysul, 1991), p. 78.

134-135   *South Wales Daily News*, 18 December 1905.

136   *Western Mail*, 1 January 1901.

137   'We have won...' *Y Tyst* quoted in translation in, John S. Ellis, 'Reconciling the Celt: British national identity, empire, and the 1911 investiture of the Prince of Wales', *Journal of British Studies*, 37, 4 (1998), 391-418, p. 400.

137-138   T. W. H. Crosland, *Taffy was a Welshman* (London, 1912), pp.12-13.

139   H. V. Morton, *In Search of Wales* (London, 1932), p. 46.

141   *Report of the Boundary Commissioners of England and Wales 1888*, p. 315.

141   Zimmern quoted in Dai Smith, *Wales: A Question for History* (Bridgend, 1999), pp. 139-40.

144   Epynt minister: Herbert Hughes, *An Uprooted Community: A History of Epynt* (Llandysul, 1998), p. 98.

147-148   W. H. Mainwaring and Aneurin Bevan quoted in Martin Johnes, *Wales since 1939* (Manchester, 1939), p. 47.

148   Linda Colley, Britishness in the 21st Century, Talk at LSE, 8 December 1999. Online at: https://www.centreforcitizenship.org/docs/britishness.pdf

150   Iorwerth Peate in *The Times*, 30 July 1957.

151   Letters to government held at National Archives: BD 24/174.

152   'it's all going to England...' in James Morris, 'Welshness in Wales', *Wales*, 1 (September 1958), p. 18.

152   David Llewellyn in *The Times*, 30 July 1957.

153   Comments to government and Gwynfor Evans quoted in Rhys Evans, *Gwynfor: Portrait of a Patriot* (Talybont, 2008), ch. 6.

155   Richard Crossman, *The Diaries of a Cabinet Minister, vol. 1* (London, 1975), p. 117.

160-161 *South Wales Echo*, 1 and 3 March 1979.

166   Sir Goronwy Owen in *Hansard*, 28 December 1945.

176   R. S. Thomas, 'Welsh landscape', in *Collected Poems 1945–1990* (London, 2000), p. 37.

SELECT BIBLIOGRAPHY

A full bibliography would, in many ways, be everything I have read over the last two decades. Here I list the most useful introductions to Welsh history and works I found useful for specific sections of my text.

Aaron, Jane and Chris Williams (eds), *Postcolonial Wales* (Cardiff, 2005).

Anderson, Benedict, *Imagined Communities: Reflections on the Origin and Spread of Nationalism* (London, 1991).

ap Glyn, Ifor, "Dear Mother, I am very sorry I cannot write to you in Welsh ...': Censorship and the Welsh language in the First World War', in Julian Walker and Christophe Declercq (eds), *Languages and the First World War: Communicating in a Transnational War* (London, 2016), pp. 128–41.

Bartlett, Robert, *The Making of Europe: Conquest, Colonization and Cultural Change 950-1350* (London, 1993).

Beddoe, Deidre, *Out of the Shadows: A History of Women in Twentieth-Century Wales* (Cardiff, 2000).

Bohata, Kirsti, *Postcolonialism Revisited: Writing Wales in English* (Cardiff, 2004).

Bowen, H. V. (ed), *Wales and the British Overseas Empire: Interactions and Influences, 1680-1830* (Manchester, 2011).

Bowen, H. V. (ed), *A New History of Wales: Myths and Realities in Welsh History* (Llandysul, 2011).

Bowen, Ivor, *The Statutes of Wales* (London, 1908).

Brady, Lindy, *Writing the Welsh Borderlands in Anglo-Saxon England* (Manchester, 2017).

Brooks, Simon, *Why Wales Never Was: The Failure of Welsh Nationalism* (Cardiff, 2017).

Burge, Alun, 'The Mold riots of 1869', *Llafur*, 3, 3 (1982), 42-57.

Cannadine, David, 'British history as a "new subject": politics, perspectives and prospects', in Alexander Grant and Keith J. Stringer (eds), *Uniting the Kingdom? The Making of British History* (London, 1995), 12-28.

Cavell, Emma, 'Widows, native law and the long shadow of England in thirteenth-century Wales', *English Historical Review*, 335 (2018).

Charles-Edwards, *Wales and the Britons 350-1064* (Oxford, 2013).

Colley, Linda, *Britons: Forging the Nation, 1707-1837* (London, 1992).

Cragoe, Matthew, 'A question of culture: the Welsh church and the bishopric of Saint-Asaph, 1870', *Welsh History Review*, 18 (1996), 228-54.

Cragoe, Matthew, *Culture, Politics and National Identity in Wales 1832-1886* (Oxford, 2004).

Cragoe, Matthew, 'Wales', in Chris Williams (ed), *A Companion to Nineteenth-Century Britain* (Oxford, 2007), pp. 521-33.

Cragoe, Matthew & Chris Williams (eds), *Wales and War: Society, Politics and Religion in the Nineteenth and Twentieth Centuries* (Cardiff, 2007).

Davies, Janet, *The Welsh Language: A History* (Cardiff, 2014).

Davies, John, *A History of Wales* (London, 1993).

Davies, R. R., 'Colonial Wales,' *Past and Present,* 65 (1974), 3-23.

Davies, R. R. *The Age of Conquest: Wales 1063-1415* (Oxford, 1987).

Davies, R. R., *Owain Glyn Dŵr: Prince of Wales* (Talybont, 2009).

Davies, R. R., *The First English Empire: Power and Identities in the British Isles, 1093-1343* (Oxford, 2003).

Davies, R. R. & Geraint H. Jenkins (eds), *From Medieval to Modern Wales: Historical Essays in Honour of Kenneth O. Morgan and Ralph A. Griffiths* (Cardiff, 2004).

Davies, Russell, *Hope and Heartbreak: A Social History of Wales and the Welsh, 1776-1871* (Cardiff, 2005).

Davies, Russell, *'Pain and Pleasure': A Social History of Wales and the Welsh, 1870-1945*. 2 volumes (Cardiff, 2015 & 2018).

Davies, Sean, *The Last King of Wales: Gruffudd ap Llywelyn c.1013-63* (Stroud, 2012).

Edwards, Owen M., *Wales* (London, 1901).

Ellis, John S., 'Reconciling the Celt: British national identity, empire, and the 1911 investiture of the Prince of Wales', *Journal of British Studies*, 37, 4 (1998), 391-418.

Ellis, John S., *Investiture: Royal Ceremony and National Identity in Wales, 1911-1969* (Cardiff, 2008).

Evans, Chris, *Slave Wales: The Welsh and Atlantic Slavery 1660-1850* (Cardiff, 2010).

Evans, Rhys, *Gwynfor: Portrait of a Patriot* (Talybont, 2008).

Gillingham, John, 'The beginnings of English imperialism', *Journal of Historical Sociology*, 5, 4 (1992), 392-409.

Henken, Elissa R., *National Redeemer: Owain Glyndŵr in Welsh Tradition* (Cardiff, 1996).

Herbert, Trevor & Gareth Elwyn Jones (eds), *Edward I and Wales* (Cardiff, 1988).

Hilling, John B., *The History and Architecture of Cardiff Civic Centre: Black Gold, White City* (Cardiff, 2016).

Hobsbawm, E. J., *Nations and Nationalism since 1870: Programme, Myth, Reality* (Cambridge, 1990).

Jenkins, Bethan M., *Between Wales and England: Anglophone Welsh Writing of the Eighteenth Century* (Cardiff, 2017).

Jenkins, Geraint H. (ed.), *The Welsh Language before the Industrial Revolution* (Cardiff, 1997).

Jenkins, Geraint H. (ed.), *The Welsh Language and its Social Domains 1801-1911* (Cardiff, 2000).

Jenkins, Geraint H. & Mari A. Williams (eds), *'Let's Do Our Best for the Ancient Tongue': The Welsh Language in the Twentieth Century* (Cardiff, 2000).

Jenkins, Geraint H. *The Foundations of Early Modern Wales, 1642-1780* (Oxford, 1993).

Jenkins, Geraint H., 'Clio and Wales: Welsh remembrancers and historical writing, 1751-2001', *Transactions of the Honourable Society of Cymmrodorion*, 8 (2001), 119-36.

Jenkins, Geraint H., *A Concise History of Wales* (Cambridge, 2007).

Jenkins, Philip, *A History of Modern Wales, 1536-1990* (Harlow, 1992).

Jenkins, Philip. 'Seventeenth-century Wales: definition and identity', in Brendan Bradshaw & Peter Roberts (eds), *British Consciousness and Identity: The Making of Britain, 1533-1707* (Oxford, 1998), pp. 213-35.

John, Mary, 'Where are the Flemings?', Pembrokeshire Historical Society (2016). Available online at http://www.pembrokeshirehistoricalsociety.co.uk/where-are-the-flemings/

Johnes, Martin, *Soccer and Society: South Wales 1900-39* (Cardiff, 2002).

Johnes, Martin, 'A Prince, a king, and a referendum: rugby, politics, and nationhood in Wales, 1969–1979', *Journal of British Studies*, 47, 1 (2008), 129-48.

Johnes, Martin, *Wales since 1939* (Manchester, 2012).

Johns, Susan M., *Gender, Nation and Conquest in the High Middle Ages: Nest of Deheubarth* (Manchester, 2013).

Jones, Aled, *Press, Politics and Society: A History of Journalism in Wales* (Cardiff, 1993).

Jones, David J. V., 'More light on "Rhyfel y Sais Bach"', *Ceredigion*, 5 (1964).

Jones, Gareth Elwyn, *A History of Education in Wales* (Cardiff, 2003).

Jones, Gareth Elwyn & Dai Smith (eds), *The People of Wales* (Llandysul, 1999).

Jones, Ieuan Gwynedd, *Mid-Victorian Wales: The Observers and the Observed* (Cardiff, 1992).

Jones, J. Gwynfor, *Early Modern Wales, c.1525-1640* (Basingstoke, 1994).

Jones, R. Merfyn, *The North Wales Quarrymen 1874-1922* (Cardiff, 1999).

Jones, R Merfyn. 'Beyond identity? The reconstruction of the Welsh'. *Journal of British Studies,* 31 (1992).

Jones, Richard Wyn, *Rhoi Cymru'n Gyntaf: Syniadaeth Plaid Cymru* (Caerdydd, 2007).

Jones, W. D. & Aled Jones, 'The Welsh world and the British Empire, c.1851-1939: an exploration', *Journal of Imperial & Commonwealth History*, 31, 2 (2003), 57-81.

Jones, Watcyn L., *Cofio Capel Celyn* (Llandysul, 2007).

Leslie, Stephen et al, 'The fine-scale genetic structure of the British population', *Nature*, 519 (2015), 309-14.

Lieberman, Max, *The March of Wales, 1067-1300* (Cardiff, 2008).

Mackenzie, John, 'Irish, Scottish, Welsh and English worlds? A four-nation approach to the history of the British empire', *History Compass*, 6, 5 (2008), 1244-63.

Milward, E. G., *Cendl o Bobl Ddewrion: Agweddau ar Lenyddiaeth Oes Victoria* (Llandysul, 1991).

Morgan, Kenneth O., *Rebirth of a Nation, Wales, 1880-1980* (Oxford, 1981).

Morgan, Kenneth O., *Revolution to Devolution: Reflections on Welsh Democracy* (Cardiff, 2014).

Morgan, Prys, 'From a death to a view: the hunt for the Welsh past in the romantic period', in Eric Hobsbawm & Terence Ranger (eds), *The Invention of Tradition* (Cambridge, 1983), pp. 43-100.

Oppenheimer, Stephen, *The Origins of the British: A Genetic Detective Story* (London, 2006).

Phillips, Dylan, *Trwy Ddullia Chwyldro...? Hanes Cymdeithas yr Iaith Gymraeg, 1962-1992* (Llandysul, 1998).

Pryce, Huw, 'British or Welsh? National identity in twelfth-century Wales', *English Historical Review*, 116, 468 (2001), 775-801.

Roberts, Gwyneth Tyson, *The Language of the Blue Books: The Perfect Instrument of Empire* (Cardiff, 1998).

Smith, Dai, *Wales! Wales?* (London, 1984).

Smith, Dai, *Wales: A Question for History* (Bridgend, 1999).

Stevens, Matthew Frank, *Urban Assimilation in Post-Conquest Wales: Ethnicity, Gender and Economy in Ruthin, 1282-1348* (Cardiff, 2010).

Sykes, Bryan, *Blood of the Isles* (London, 2007).

Taylor, Lucy, 'Welsh–indigenous relationships in nineteenth century Patagonia: 'Friendship' and the coloniality of power', *Journal of Latin American Studies*, 49, 1 (2017), 143-68.

Taylor, Lucy, 'Global perspectives on Welsh Patagonia: the complexities of being both colonizer and colonized', *Journal of Global History*, 13, 3 (2018), 446-68.

Thomas, Hugh, *Wales, 1485-1660* (Cardiff, 1972).

Thomas, M. Wynn, *The Nations of Wales, 1890-1914* (Cardiff, 2016).

Thomas, Wyn, *Hands off Wales: Nationhood and Militancy* (Llandysul, 2013).

Watkin, Thomas Glyn, *The Legal History of Wales* (Cardiff, 2007).

Williams, Charlotte, Neil Evans & Paul O'Leary (eds), *A Tolerant Nation? Exploring Ethnic Diversity in Wales* (Cardiff, 2003).

Williams, Chris, *Capitalism, Community and Conflict: The South Wales Coalfield, 1898-1947* (Cardiff, 1998).

Williams, Chris, 'Who talks of my nation?' in Chris Williams & Andy Croll (eds), *The Gwent County History. Vol. 5: The Twentieth Century* (Cardiff, 2013), pp. 342-62.

Williams, Daniel, *Wales Unchained: Literature, Politics and Identity in the American Century* (Cardiff, 2015).

Williams, Gareth, *1905 and all that: Essays on Rugby Football, Sport and Welsh Society* (Llandysul, 1991).

Williams, Glanmor, *Renewal and Reformation: Wales, c.1415– 1642* (Oxford, 1987).

Williams, Glanmor, *Wales and the Reformation* (Cardiff, 1997).

Williams, Gwyn A., *When was Wales? A History of the Welsh* (London, 1985).

Williams, John, *Was Wales Industrialised? Essays in Modern Welsh History* (Llandysul, 1995).

Williams, Tim, 'The Anglicisation of south Wales', in Raphael Samuel (ed.), *Patriotism: The Making and Unmaking of British National Identity, vol. II: Minorities and Outsiders* (London, 1989), pp. 197-201.

Wright, Martin, *Wales and Socialism: Political Culture and National Identity before the Great War* (Cardiff, 2016)

INDEX

SMOOTH OPERATOR

Geoff Andrews

Cyril Lakin was the epitome of a smooth operator. From a humble background in Barry, Cyril Lakin studied at Oxford, survived the first world war, and went on to become a Fleet Street editor, radio presenter and war-time member of parliament. As literary editor of both the *Daily Telegraph* and the *Sunday Times*, Lakin was at the centre of a vibrant and radical generation of writers, poets and critics.

Geoff Andrews brings a fresh perspective to the life and times of a fascinating man who was involved in the national story at a time of great change for the United Kingdom and Wales.

HB / £20
978-1-913640-18-7

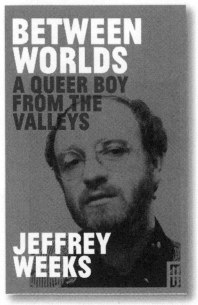

BETWEEN WORLDS: A QUEER BOY FROM THE VALLEYS

Jeffrey Weeks

A man's own story from the Rhondda. Jeffrey Weeks was born in the Rhondda in 1945, of mining stock. As he grew up he increasingly felt an outsider in the intensely community-minded valleys, a feeling intensified as he became aware of his gayness. Escape came through education. He left for London, to university, and to realise his sexuality. He has been described as the 'most significant British intellectual working on sexuality to emerge from the radical sexual movements of the 1970s'.

HB / £20
978-1-912681-88-4

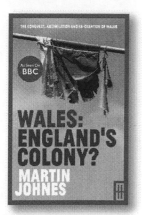

WALES: ENGLAND'S COLONY?

Martin Johnes

From the very beginnings of Wales, its people have defined themselves against their large neighbour. This book tells the fascinating story of an uneasy and unequal relationship between two nations living side-by-side.

PB / £8.99
978-1-912681-41-9

RHYS DAVIES: A WRITER'S LIFE

Meic Stephens

Rhys Davies (1901-78) was among the most dedicated, prolific and accomplished of Welsh prose writers. This is his first full biography.

'This is a delightful book, which is itself a social history in its own right, and funny.'
– The Spectator

PB / £11.99
978-1-912109-96-8

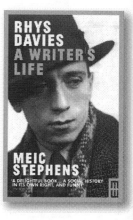

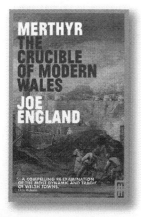

MERTHYR, THE CRUCIBLE OF MODERN WALES

Joe England

Merthyr Tydfil was the town where the future of a country was forged: a thriving, struggling surge of people, industry, democracy and ideas. This book assesses an epic history of Merthyr from 1760 to 1912 through the focus of a fresh and thoroughly convincing perspective.

PB / £18.99
978-1-913640-05-7

TO HEAR THE SKYLARK'S SONG

Huw Lewis

To Hear the Skylark's Song is a memoir about how Aberfan survived and eventually thrived after the terrible disaster of the 21st of October 1966.

'A thoughtful and passionate memoir, moving and respectful.'
– Tessa Hadley

PB / £8.99
978-1-912109-72-2

ROCKING THE BOAT

Angela V. John

This insightful and revealing collection of essays focuses on seven Welsh women who, in a range of imaginative ways, resisted the status quo in Wales, England and beyond during the nineteenth and twentieth centuries.

PB / £11.99
978-1-912681-44-0

TURNING THE TIDE

Angela V. John

This rich biography tells the remarkable tale of Margaret Haig Thomas (1883-1958) who became the second Viscountess Rhondda. She was a Welsh suffragette, held important posts during the First World War and survived the sinking of the *Lusitania*.

PB / £17.99
978-1-909844-72-8

BRENDA CHAMBERLAIN, ARTIST & WRITER

Jill Piercy

The first full-length biography of Brenda Chamberlain chronicles the life of an artist and writer whose work was strongly affected by the places she lived, most famously Bardsey Island and the Greek island of Hydra.

PB / £11.99
978-1-912681-06-8